When Our Love Is Not Enough

Chapters

Introduction

1. How Did I Get Here
2. It All Started with Respite
3. Making The Transitions
4. Love in the Face of Emotions
5. Love in the Face of Identity
6. Love in the Face of Rejection
7. Love in the Face of Loss
8. Love in the Face of Family Dynamics
9. Love in the Face of Fear
10. Love in the Face of Dreams
11. Love in the Face of Mistakes
12. Love in the Face of Death
13. Love in the Face of Grief
14. Love in the Face of Determination
15. Dear Police Officer
16. Dear Neighbors and Community
17. Do not Give Up On Me

Acknowledgments

I would like to thank the following:

- The young adults who have allowed me to share a part of their story
- My friends who supported and encouraged me throughout this journey
- My friend, Joy, who blessed me with a quiet mountain spot to write
- My Beta Readers
    - Wendy Lyman
    - Jessica Lloyd-Rogers
    - Daniel Pasono
    - Rebecca Parkinson
    - Andrew Sawyer
- Robyn Kelly – Loop Creative – Book design cover and back
- My husband Jim – thank you for being my rock and support

Forward

This book is dedicated to each and every young person who has crossed my threshold, whether for a few hours or for years. Whether you realize it or not, you have each placed a footprint on my heart that will never be the same. This book is about you, about your resilience, about your dedication, about your struggles, about your successes. I could not include every one of you and every story I wanted to tell but hopefully this is just the first book, and more is to come.

Thank you each for letting me share your journey to help bring change to a system that has severely failed each one of you. May the scars that each of you allowed me to share, help bring awareness and healing to many. I love you all immensely and will forever be grateful for all you have taught me. Mama

Introduction

I set out to write this book to share stories and events that have taken place over the 23 years of building a family in our home. Our family is unconventional, not built out of my womb, but out of my heart. I am sharing with you my journey and how my heart has been captured by young adults who have aged out of the foster care system. The journey has not been easy for me, even more so for them, but I would not change it for anything.

So much stirs in me for kids who have been and are in foster care. They are often misunderstood and treated as though they, themselves, made the decisions to be where they are today. The battles they each face from the years of being mistreated, tossed from home to home, and the experiences they have, fill my heart with compassion. To be honest, there is often anger in me as I hear many of their stories, but my heart is to love everyone unconditionally, watch them overcome life's challenges, and make decisions for themselves.

These stories not only bear the truth about their struggles but also declare the victories, for many. Their journeys are not easy. The behaviors and actions often exhibited are a product of years of abuse and hurt, not rebellion and disrespect. I want to help you put on a different lens, see what is truly taking place, and understand how we can come together to help these kids.

Learning to understand and support these young people, while putting aside my feelings, has been one of my biggest challenges. It has also been important to make sure I have healthy outlets to express my own emotions and work through my thoughts and feelings.

When I meet people and the topic of fostering comes up, there is usually one question and one statement included in the conversation. How did you get into fostering? And -

I could never be a foster parent, my heart could not take giving the kids back. My heartfelt hope for this book is to share my journey and encourage foster parents along the way. It is intended for foster parents, kids in care, and the community at large, as we all play a role in the lives of these young people, whether we realize it or not.

Some stories are going to be from my perspective, some from what I perceive to be my kids' perspective. There will be events that break your heart, and others will help you realize that there is so much more to foster parenting than just in the moment. It truly takes more than love, love for kids, love for parenting, love for…, you name it.

I will also talk a little about how we, as foster parents, are often overlooked and feel like we are not important to the kids or the system. It seems that how we feel and what we see does not matter. My faith lies in the fact that it does. Based upon the testimonies of young adults who have been in my care and the differences that I see, as well as hearing them talk about, I know that it takes time. I want to encourage foster parents to keep an eye on those kids they have right now. Hold them close and the rest will take care of itself. Situations are not always going to look the way we want them to, and some may not have a good or happy ending, but knowing the impact and love that you give to these young people, while they are in your care, makes a huge difference.

At the end of each chapter, I will talk about tools that have helped me in these moments. Tools that you can engage and help, not only you but the young adults as well. Being able to face these situations, equipped with discernment and understanding, brings a level of safety to you and them.

The struggles are real, but they are even more real for these kids and, as a parent, we must keep that in mind.

While circumstances may appear to be bad, at the moment, give yourself a few years and you will truly see the fruit of everything you have done. Take this journey with me as I share stories of what I have faced and done and stories about some of the kids and young adults who have been in my home over the last 23 years. I hope that you enjoy it, as we learn more tools and discover what is deep in every young person you love, even when it is not enough.

**Chapter 1
How Did I Get Here**

One of the most significant God moments of my life led me to foster parenting. Some of you may think I am crazy and others it may cause you to tear up. Trust me, this event changed the trajectory of my life in such a significant way, and the words spoken to me by the Lord are forever implanted in my soul. Grab your coffee and let this moment touch your heart and know that, while not all of us will have an experience like this, kids, teens, and young adults are crying out for our help and love.

It was the year of my 31st birthday. I was going through a very difficult time personally, one that I had faced many times over as a single woman. My heart was so empty and lonely and tired of feeling lost. From the outside looking in, life looked perfect. I had a great corporate job as an accountant and had been working my way up within the company, living in three states and working in management. My house was big enough that I had two single mothers and their three kids living with me. I was active in my community, volunteering for various organizations and having fun while doing it, as well as active in my church family. How could I be feeling so lonely and empty with all of that?

As most women do, I dreamt of the perfect husband with the perfect house, perfect neighbors, and perfect kids. While I had the perfect neighbors and house down pat, the missing husband and kids far outweighed those facts. Even my job did not fulfill my heart. I felt like there was something more that I was supposed to be doing but just could not put my finger on what that was. Even with volunteering and engaging in my church, serving others, and helping build a community, something was still missing.

I got to the point where I felt like I was falling into depression and could not take the emptiness anymore. My heart was so unfulfilled I decided that I needed to do something serious about it. Feeling compelled to fast and pray for a few days, I set out to take a week and do so. I do not remember which day I was in the fast, but what I do remember is the heart of desperation that I was feeling. It was a rare moment that I had the house to myself, so I put on some instrumental music that provided an atmosphere of peace and meditation and sat on the floor with my bible and notebook. Before I knew it, I was face down on my floor in complete tears. As I cried out to God weeping, a feeling of peace overtook me. Suddenly, I heard what sounded like a tugboat coming into the harbor bringing in a shipment. What in the world? I thought, confused by what I was hearing. I sat up startled and looked out my windows to see what was going on. There was absolutely nothing but complete silence outside. I laid back down on the floor, still feeling a sense of peace. Again, I heard the tugboat sound, so I sat up and grabbed my journal. As I sat there writing the words that came to my heart, I was overcome by His presence. "I will bring boatloads of kids into your life and greater is the impact that you will have on them than any that could come from your womb," were the exact words that He spoke to me. I sat there continuing to journal, tears streaming down my cheeks as I did so. Soon He asked me to read Isaiah 54. These words tore me to pieces and felt like they were put there just for me.

"Sing, O barren woman,
You who have not borne!
Break forth into singing, and cry aloud,
You who have not labored with child!
For more are the children of the desolate
Then the children of the married woman," says the Lord.
"Enlarge the place of your tent,
And let them stretch out the curtains of your dwellings.

> Do not spare:
> Lengthen your cords,
> And strengthen your stakes.
> For you shall expand to the right and to the left.
> And your descendants will inherit the nations,
> And make the desolate cities inhabited.
> Do not fear, for you will not be ashamed;
> Neither be disgraced, for you will not be put to shame;
> For you will forget the shame of your youth,
> And will not remember the reproach of your widowhood anymore.
> For your Maker is your husband,
> The Lord of hosts is His name."

As I continued my fast for the next few days God began to reprimand me, and how I had let go of my dreams. For some, the use of the word reprimand may be a little harsh but quite often, when we look on the other side of it, there are usually lessons learned and growth that comes as a result. He took me back to dreams that I once had, dreams of making a difference that involved kids. Some dreams were smaller than others but most of them had been put on the shelf for later.

Later? Yeah later, as in when that perfect man came along, then all these dreams would magically come off the shelf and suddenly become relevant again – not so much! One of the dreams that I remember was when I was about to graduate from college.

When I first started my studies, I wanted to be a special education teacher, but I graduated with an accounting degree. I know that this is a major transition, but to be honest, my heart never changed regarding children. Throughout college, I worked in group homes with kids to help me financially. I also volunteered in a couple of organizations that involved kids.

As I prepared to graduate college I began to think about my future, trying to decide where to go next. As I started to consider the Peace Corps, I began to envision myself going to Africa and working with kids in an orphanage. I joked all the time that if I ever went to Africa, or anywhere with kids, I would come back with my suitcase full of kids and leave my belongings there. While my parents probably do not remember this, we had a discussion one day about it and they expressed concern, so I decided to let it go, pretty much as quickly as it started.

But this time was different. While I was not looking to join the Peace Corps or some other organization, the cry in my heart was becoming stronger and stronger for kids. God spoke to me about how I had put those dreams on the shelf in hopes that when love came, my dreams would suddenly come true. Instead, He said, "No, love will come through you serving these kids." And so began my journey.

The next few weeks, what God had been speaking to me continued to weigh heavy on my heart. As I prayed and sought Him for my next steps, doors began to suddenly open.

It was the holiday season and I served on a committee at work that did outreach in our community. I had taken on the assignment of finding a family that we could support over the holiday season. I started in the Yellow Pages. Does anybody remember those? For those who do not, we used to use a phone book not only to look up a friend's phone number but quite often to search for a business that would meet a need, like an electrician, plumber, phone company, or just about anything. I do not remember what category I turned to but suddenly, words jumped off the page at me – Volunteer Families for Children – hmm, I thought, I wonder what this organization is about? I quickly scribbled down the name and phone number to investigate later and continued my journey to find the family for our company.

After finding an organization through which we could sponsor our family, I finished up the phone calls related to that and then decided to dial the number I jotted down.

As I started my conversation with the woman on the phone, something new began to spark in my heart. She explained that they helped families who were at risk of losing their kids to the foster care system. To volunteer, I would have to complete the training to get a foster parent license and then I would be able to provide care. We discussed different options of what that care would look like as I was a single person with a full-time job and wanted to make sure everything went well. As I went through the training, we began talking about what role I could fill, deciding that providing respite to foster families and weekend care to kids in their program was where I would start.

As I look back, I truly did not know the depth of the love that I would have for these kids and their families. I discover new depths every day as I continue to be involved in foster care in many ways. I have served babies to young adults and every one of them not only holds a special place in my heart but each one has also taught me a different lesson. While the lessons have been different, the common ground that each has had is, love is not enough.

Chapter 2
It All Started with Respite

Over the 20-plus years I have been fostering, I have had over 80 kids in my home. The reason I have had so many is that I primarily provided respite and preventative care for the first 3 or 4 years. Respite is to give foster families an occasional break from the kids in their homes. This may be for a weekend or a week, depending on what the needs are. Quite often it was while families were on vacation and the kids in their care were not able or allowed to go with them.

Preventative care was helping families that were at risk of their kids being put into foster care by giving them a break. Providing this care has given me long-term relationships, as well as brought multiple kids from babies to young adults.

There are so many stories I can tell from these experiences and some of them will be captured in this book. When I first started helping these families, I realized most of them were single mothers. I ventured out to start an organization to help women at risk of losing their kids to foster care, but my heart kept getting pulled toward the kids.

One young man, whom I took care of in the early years, is Eric. I still have a relationship with Eric and his family, even after more than 15 years. When Eric first came into my care, his mother needed help with her two kids for various reasons. Our goal was to provide support to avoid her kids being put into foster care, which we successfully did. Eric would come and spend weekends with us monthly. At the time, I had two friends from church, and their kids, living with me. Gail and Angela were very supportive of me becoming a foster parent so, they too got licensed to help provide care to kids. Gail continued to foster parents for a short period after she and her daughter moved into their own home. They had one of the most adorable little girls in their care for a while as well as a few other joys.

Navigating through being foster parents and parenting together, with Gail and Angela, brought a few challenges. Honestly, I think that anybody who parents together in any way hits challenges, right? Typically, we worked through them pretty smoothly, but there is one event that we often laugh about, even to this day. As a seasoned foster parent, I now realize how uptight I was as a new one. We could not follow the rules more than we did as I was a real stickler, to say the least. Most of the time I would not let the kids in our care out of my sight because I wanted to make sure that everything was okay, and we were doing what we were supposed to. It was rare that I would leave anybody in Gail and/or Angela's care, for fear that something might happen, even though they had children of their own. Children whom they had raised as single mothers and were amazing kids.

One day, I had some errands I had to do, so I left Eric in the care of Angela. Her kids were the same age as Eric and got along extremely well. Upon my return home, I discovered that Angela was home, but Eric was nowhere to be found. According to our agency's rules, the kids in our care were "not to be out of our sight," and I lost it. Angela told me that she let them go out for a walk and they had been gone for about an hour. I immediately went into panic mode and set out to find them. As I was getting ready to pull out of the driveway, the three kids came walking down the sidewalk, laughing, and having a fantastic time with each other, just being kids. I will honestly say that it took me a few days to calm down about this situation and a few years to get to the point where I could laugh about how ridiculous I was. It is unfortunate that the foster system makes us feel this way by instilling fear and often making kids feel like they cannot have normal lives. Eric was not in harm's way. He was perfectly fine, enjoying time with his friends. I just needed to relax.

I had a similar experience a few years later when I was parenting on my own. One of my kids called and asked if he could go to the pool with his friend. I told him, that if his friend's mom or grandma was going with them, that was fine. When I returned home from work that afternoon, the young man in my care was nowhere to be found. I went to his friend's house and his grandma informed me she had been told they would be at my home. They had pulled a fast one on both of us.

Grandma and I split up and started searching for the boys. Eventually, two sub-divisions from us, I found the boys at the pool with a group of kids. I stormed into that pool area and demanded the two of them get in the car NOW! I look back and think what a fool I made myself and the boys look. Again, they were just being normal 12-year-old boys, and I was being an overreactive parent. He did not get taken from me because of this situation and he and I still laugh about it to this day. I am positive that this boy is not the only young man in this world who has done such a thing, and I am not the only parent who reacted in such a manner.

The struggle is real when you become a foster parent. You feel like you always have this magnifying glass over you and your kids. At one point I even thought that one of the social workers was spying on me. I was so paranoid I thought they had a camera in the gazebo across from my house and went over to check it out. How ridiculous is that?

So often, the feeling is, I cannot make any mistakes as a parent or I am going to lose the kids, or even worse lose my license. Eric and the young man are just two of those times that I absolutely lost it and went overboard emotionally regarding something that one of my kids did that honestly, is just being a kid. We cannot expect ourselves, as foster parents, or our kids to be perfect in any way shape, or form. Honestly, we should not expect this from any parent, and I often think that kids are taken from their birth parents' way too soon for this very reason. Do not misunderstand me, there are reasons that kids should be taken away for their protection, but too many times they are just taken because of a difference one might have in the way they choose to parent. There is so much going on in the system right now to help with this because it causes so much heartache, especially for the kids. I hope some changes can be made sooner rather than later.

Another one of my respite stories that I like to share, and shows the impact that we, as foster parents, have on kids is about two sisters. I was helping a single mother who was struggling with an addiction to not have her girls taken from her. The girls came and stayed with me for a month while their mother attended a treatment program. We continued to have a relationship for a few years, and the girls would come to spend the weekend with me from time to time. They would also call me to talk as would their mom. Sometimes, I would go see them and their mother and we would do activities together. Two events I specifically remember are going blueberry picking and going to see fireworks. We used to have so much fun together and built a great relationship.

It had been a few years since I heard from them or their mother, and we had lost touch. I received a phone call from another state asking if I was Maurita. I confirmed I was, and the woman on the phone explained that the two girls were in the state's custody and were about to be adopted by a family. The girls asked if she would contact me for some pictures. I got her email and shared what I could find, as well as my contact information, expressing that I would love to hear from the girls. That was the last that I heard but knowing how the girls felt, and that they thought of me meant so much. I think of so many of the kids I have had regularly and hope that every one of them is thriving and that things have gone well for them.

I really cannot resist sharing this little story with you as well. There was a little boy who spent the weekend with me once a month.

On Friday he was scheduled to come, and I was needing to stay at work to get some things done. The social worker dropped him off at my office. While I worked, he wrote on my whiteboard, drew pictures, and did other things to keep himself busy for a couple of hours.

Once we were in the car and on the way home, I looked in the back seat and thanked him for being so good. I told him that, since he did so well, I was going to let him decide where we would go for dinner. He sat there, looking out the window, thinking about it. Soon I heard, "Pizza, I want some pizza!" "Well, pizza it is," I replied.

The ride continued in silence for a few minutes as he appeared to be in thought. Me, thinking it was about what kind of pizza he was going to get, was taken by the words that soon came out of his mouth. "Ms. Maurita?" "Yes," I replied. "You make my heart feel good!" How precious is that? Those words keep me going even today.

Love is one of the greatest gifts we have to offer kids as foster parents. It is that love that often feels trampled on and unappreciated by the system, the kids, parents, and even the community. We do not claim to be perfect and many of us try so hard to help support the birth families with reunification or other solutions. My heart and concern were because of the love that I have for these kids, but that often gets blinded by the rules and regulations set before me. It even, sometimes, put up a wall between me and the kids because they felt like I was too strict or stern. This is another aspect that I do not think only we as foster parents have. All parents face the walls due to the rules and protection we put around kids but often in foster parenting that is thrown back into our faces. As we try to do certain things, words like, "You are not my mom!" will fly. We just have to keep holding on, not let the words get the best of us, and do our best. I look back today and realize how I felt like the fact that I loved and cared for them was not enough, at the time. Looking at things now, I know that it was not, it takes more than love.

Chapter 3
Making the Transitions

Serving kids has brought many transitions in my life. Each of these transitions deepened my love, opened my awareness, and brought me to where I am today, serving young adults.

When I started fostering, by providing respite services, I honestly did not consider anything beyond that, but one day I received the call that started changing everything. My social worker had four kids who needed a home willing to work with their mother for reunification. The first step was to move the kids into one home together. The two girls were placed in a separate home from their baby brothers and were having a hard time. Having the kids in one home helped provide stability and was easier to coordinate visits and activities with Mom.

Upon receiving the call, I reached out to my friends, and we quickly converted my home with cribs, beds, food, and more. Having the support was so important, and I look back, knowing I could not have done it without my church family. It was Saturday morning, and the kids were going to be dropped off later in the afternoon. I remember a bunch of friends were at my house and I was sitting on the dining room floor scraping paint off the floor with my fingernail. One of my friends saw me and asked if I was OK. I broke a few tears, concerned over whether I would be a good mom for these kids. I knew nothing about them except that they had been separated and were excited to come back together. Making a transition from zero to four kids was huge, especially doing it by myself and with a full-time job.

I often talk about this time, as this was my first transition, going from respite to full-time fostering. I honestly have not had an empty house for long since then. Whenever I talk about it, I often say that it was the craziest time of my life but also the best. Every morning I had three places I had to drop the kids off, taking me over two hours to get to work. The afternoon was easier, as the daycare the boys were at would pick up the two girls from school, making it so I could pick them all up together. This foursome was with me for about nine months, quickly being reunited with their mother, bringing joy to everyone. While they were with me, we spent regular time with Mom, having her join us for birthdays, trick or treating, Christmas or just going to the park. I have lost touch with these kids and their mom, but believe me, my heart has not. I think of them regularly.

The next major transition was changing from fostering young kids to fostering teenagers. This one came with the blessing of my daughter, Priscilla. Priscilla was 12 years old when I met her. Not only was I now fostering teenagers, but it was the first time I seriously considered adoption. Priscilla had been in the system since she was about five years old. She had had no contact with either of her parents and was wanting a forever home, as was her sister, Hannah. It was decided that it would be best if they each had their own place to call home, and Hannah had been placed with a family that was already preparing to adopt her. Priscilla had been told that she had three families that was going to visit, and after those visits, she could make a choice as to which one she wanted.

We scheduled a long weekend for her to come to visit me. We spent the weekend getting to know each other, playing games, talking, taking walks, and just being together. We also attended church, where she was immediately embraced and loved by many. It was like putting on Cinderella's shoes, it only fit me. Priscilla and I had so much fun together and neither of us wanted the weekend to end. She felt like she belonged, and we had been a part of each other's lives forever. Upon returning to her home, she called and told her social worker she did not need to visit the other homes, she wanted to live with me. A few months later Priscilla moved in.

Having Priscilla opened my eyes to the needs of teenagers. She also opened my heart to a love I never realized I had. Growing up, the teenage years were so difficult for me, I never thought I would desire to have teens in my home, but seeing Priscilla and her friends, and what they were going through made me realize how much they needed unconditional love and patience.

How young women perceive themselves often grieves my heart. I know how I felt growing up and I did not have the stigma of being a foster child on top of it. The challenge of being a teenager is already difficult. Priscilla and her friends often talked about the constant voices in their heads telling them, "Nobody loves you" and "You are ugly", just to name two. Priscilla dealt with these too, but on top of that, she also dealt with the rejection. Being in foster care for seven years and being tossed from family to family brings with it a multitude of thoughts, the biggest one being "I do not belong." The number of kids I have had in my home demonstrates this struggle is real. The face of it varies for each one of them, but the root is the fear of being rejected again. They will push and push because they do not want to get close, but at the same time lay in my arms crying because they need the comfort of someone they know who cares. These varying emotions are so real. Finding that I was able to provide a safe place for these young people to love and be loved, while at the same time screaming at the top of their lungs or pushing with the best of their strength, I decided to choose to stand with them. I chose to start fostering teens.

Along comes Kearia and Tyler, who are siblings. These two have sustained things that no person should have to sustain, especially a child. My first-time meeting Kearia and

Tyler was having them for a weekend respite. Kearia was 12 and Tyler was 10. I was nervous as all get out because Tyler has diabetes. Much like in my early days of fostering, I was so afraid I would do something wrong. I kept in contact with a friend of mine, who is a pharmacist, the whole weekend, asking questions to make sure I did not do anything wrong that would affect his health. The three of us survived the weekend unscathed, and thoroughly enjoyed our time together. About a year later, I received a phone call from my social worker asking if I would be open to Kearia coming and living with me. It broke my heart, as I knew they were trying to get the kids reunified with their mom but apparently, it did not go well.

The Kearia that arrived at my home this time was nothing like the Kearia I met a year ago. The young lady who walked in my door stood in a trance, staring and not communicating or engaging with anybody. For months all she would do was sit on the floor with her head covered with a blanket, curled in a fetal position, rocking. I tried to engage her by playing games, watching TV, doing her hair, and anything I could think of but was having no success. I cannot begin to tell you how many times I called the social worker, expressing my concerns that I was not the right placement for Kearia. Well, we stuck it out and today Kearia is now my daughter. I will be sharing more about her story later.

Tyler was placed with me about eight months after Kearia. He had been in another home, with his brother. That family had made the decision they were not interested in adoption, so Tyler decided to come and be with his sister. Two years later, I adopted them both. This past December, we celebrated 12 years of adoption. The journey has not always been easy but there is not a day that I regret the life we have built together. Have I made mistakes? You bet your bottom dollar I have, but we have walked through each of them together, building family along the way as we continue to extend our hearts to each other and other young adults.

About 10 months after Kearia moved in with me, we were introduced to another young lady, Jodie. Jodie brought the next big transition into my life. My experience with her led me to help young adults who are aging out of foster care. Her situation angered me to the point that I knew I needed to do something. In January 2010, Jodie turned 18. She had been in a foster home, along with her two babies, for some time. Once she turned 18, that home decided they did not want her staying with them any longer and forced her to leave, keeping her two boys with them. How can something like this happen? How is this fair? How is Jodie supposed to survive being torn away from her boys?

Jodie's social worker started by placing her in a home that did not go well. In March they contacted me and moved her in with Kearia and me. In North Carolina, at the time, we had, what was called, a CARS agreement. This was an agreement made between the youth and the state that they would attend school or work a certain number of hours each month to receive a stipend and remain in foster care. Jodie had chosen that option because she had nowhere to go. Seeing that she was just separated from her two sons, can you just imagine the challenge she had to meet these expectations?

I tried multiple ways to help her. We investigated getting her GED through homeschooling, going back to school, and the local community college, attempted finding her a job, had in-home counseling, and more, but nothing would motivate her to even get out of bed, much less accomplish these goals. She was in such a state of grief and shock over losing her babies.

Just a few months into her being with me, we had to go to court for her CARS agreement. We walked into the courtroom, expecting them to continue the agreement and provide us with some more time. Instead, we got a termination of that agreement.

When we arrived home later that afternoon, we were greeted at the door by the social worker who told me they had moved Kearia to another home (this event took place before her adoption). They gave me the choice of having Kearia come back or keeping Jodie, putting me in a corner to decide between my two girls. Thankfully, my neighbors, the Lyman's, stepped in and allowed Jodie to come and live with them for some time until we could get her into a safe shelter. Unable to find someone who could help her, we were forced to put her into a homeless shelter. Throughout her time there, we visited regularly, and she came home to visit. Eventually, she moved into her own apartment. Jodie got her two boys back for a few months but soon realized it was better for them to be with a family that would provide more for them. She quickly realized the challenges of providing for herself and both boys, financially and emotionally. This was a very difficult decision for Jodie, but she made the decision based on what was best for the boys. She keeps in touch with them regularly and has maintained a good relationship with them and their adoptive parents.

The next transition is Jim, my husband. When I met Jim, I had been fostering for over 15 years. I had met some men over that period, but none of them embraced the kids like Jim. Tyler is probably the biggest example of this.

Due to the abuse Tyler sustained in his life, he wanted nothing to do with another man being in the house, especially one who represented a father. Jim would come over to visit, and Tyler often responded by expressing the fact he did not want him there and would begin to be verbally aggressive and defiant. Jim did not run. He would take the time to help Tyler by talking to him, making him feel less threatened. I often joke about the fact that it took 5 years for Tyler to call me Mom but only 5 months to call Jim Dad. Today, Tyler and Jim are very close.

Jim has been an amazing addition to our family. The kids love and respect him, enjoying his dad jokes and often having discussions, especially about the bible. At the age of 51 and 48, this was the first marriage for both of us. While I had had kids in my home for years, this was a first for Jim. He instantly became a father, grandfather, uncle, and husband all in the breath of saying "I do." He often finds things to be challenging but he is willing to accept and learn from each of those challenges, serving the young adults in our lives.

I grieve when I see how kids are treated when they age out. They did not choose to be in foster care, but they are often treated as if they did. For many, I have had a sense of inadequacy, as if I were not doing any good for them. I struggled with whether my love was enough, but the bonds of love have been built as, together, we work through challenges. We have learned strategies that help all of us get through the ugly moments and hard times. Many of the kids I have had over the years are still in my life today because we stuck it out together. I am ever so grateful for the relationships we have and how they have all moved forward in their lives. We are going to share events and explain the strategy used when facing them, unveiling masks to help bring solutions.

Chapter 4
Love in the Face of Emotions

It was New Year's Day. The whole week had been a major roller coaster in our house. With seven young adults living in our home, there is often a lot of emotion. It is important to us to provide a safe environment for all the young people who join our family, no matter the length of time they are with us. We want them to know they will be loved, even during their anger and pain, even when the emotions are extremely ugly because that is what it means to be family.

I cannot begin to tell you how challenging the holidays are. Young people do not make a conscious decision about how it makes them feel, and they try so hard to stifle their emotions, many times resulting in an explosion.

My heart often breaks during this time for multiple reasons. One – all I want to do is to love each and every one of them, but so often they are not able to receive it. Two – the names I get called and the actions taken are often extremely harsh and hurt me to the core. Three – the look and longing in their eyes surrounded by a wall of protection that nobody can break through is devastating.

As I write this, we are coming out of another holiday season. Over the last two weeks, we had physical altercations due to the rampant emotions in our young adults. In my experience, so often they do not feel worthy of love, and the love I extend can be overwhelming, causing them to push me and others away. They also struggle with rejection so much more during the holidays. Their internal voices are beating them up; telling them they are not loved, do not deserve to be loved, nobody really cares, and on and on.

Last week's altercation started with one of my boys, Antony, being heartbroken over the death of one of his closest friends this year. He was having such a hard time that he turned to alcohol, hoping to numb his emotions. Instead, it exacerbated his feelings, causing him to lash out at the other young adults in the home. Fists and words flying in all directions. Jim and I tried to calm things down, but it got to the point where I had to step into my mama's authority and demand things to stop, getting in between two of the boys. Antony grabbed me by the shirt and when he looked at me, he did so in shock, realizing it was me he had grabbed. At that point, I got the two biggest players separated, which finally opened the gate for the emotions behind it all to flow. There were tears, hugs, love, and forgiveness extended, especially to the young man who was grieving.

The evening ended rather peacefully, with two of the boys talking and forgiving each other for years of the hurt they had caused each other. As they sat on the couch talking, the two girls and I went upstairs and cried together as we talked. The girls both opened up, sharing more of their stories and emotions that had been bottled up. Attempting to comfort them and express my care, stating the fact that I would be there for them, I hoped they would know how sincere I was, and that I care and love them deeply.

The next day, all hell broke loose again. One of the girls, Aech, emotionally overloaded from what happened the night before, got into a disagreement with her sister, demanding that she leave. After her sister left, Aech lashed out at me, every word ripping through my heart. The night before I expressed how sorry I was for the adults who had abandoned them and let them down. All the expressed love and emotions led to Aech pushing away the people who cared about her the most, her sister, me, and Antony. She packed up some of her belongings and sat on the front lawn for hours, saying a friend was coming to get her and we did not have to worry about her anymore. My heart was completely broken as I could see through it, but all I could do was stand there and try my best to not react to her words flying at me. I have learned that retaliation and defending myself do not work. I just needed to let her vent. Eventually, she came back into the house.

The next morning, I slid a card under her door, hoping to encourage her and let her know I cared. A few days later, she apologized, saying she did not mean anything of what she said and was sorry, I embraced her, letting her know it was okay and that I understood.

This is just one of many times I have experienced this behavior, and it will not be the last, I am sure. The biggest lesson I have learned is that I cannot take things personally. It is in these moments when I feel my love is so inadequate. I often want to quit, but I cannot. I cannot quit on these young people who have so much life to live and need love beyond what I can give. God has placed me here for this reason and it is for this reason I will forever stand – to be family.

Wikipedia defines family – "In human society, a family is a group of people related either by consanguinity or affinity. The purpose of families is to maintain the well-being of their members and society. Ideally, families would offer predictability, structure, and safety as members mature and participate in the community. In most societies, it is within families that children acquire socialization for life outside the family and act as the primary source of attachment, nurturing, and socialization for humans. Additionally, as the basic unit for meeting the basic needs of its members, it provides a sense of boundaries for performing tasks in a safe environment, ideally builds a person into a functional adult, transmits culture, and ensures the continuity of humankind with precedents of knowledge." As I read this definition, I cringed over the many breaks in this structure every young adult in our home has faced.

I do not think people understand what many of these young adult's face and how these experiences naturally result in such raw emotions. Currently, our home includes some whose parents chose drugs over them, one who lost both of his parents before he was 12, one whose parents have rejected him because of his decisions regarding his gender, one whose father is in prison and her mother was unable to care for her and her siblings on her own, and one who had such an atmosphere of contention and fighting in the home that he could not deal with it any longer. All of them have found a safe place here, knowing that no matter what they do to us we will love them.

This is not an easy decision on our part as they push our buttons regularly. We have decided to stand in the gap and watch them overcome the challenges they face and outwardly become the amazing human beings they are.

Sometimes the battles individuals fight within their heads get taken out on everyone else around them. I got a "Ms. Maurita, come get me!" call from Aech. She was fighting with Antony and wanted me to come to get her and her sisters, so they did not have to ride home with him. I arrived at the scene about 45 minutes later, the two of them still screaming and carrying on with each other. When I went to talk to Aech, she started yelling obscenities and shouting accusations and all kinds of anger and hatred at me. Every remark that came from her mouth towards me came from years of war wounds, and man, the scars are deep. The evening went on for a long time, as I attempted to get her settled down enough to come home. Finally, she got in my car, crying with her sister over the years of pain.

Often people ask me why we allow this. It is not that we allow anything, in my opinion. What we do, is give space and time for young people to receive healing, and to have a safe place to express the years of pain, as ugly as that may look. Our love can never heal every one of their scars, but we can certainly do our best for the time that God has entrusted them into our care.

I know my family of origin loves me, but even in the expression and safety of our family environment, I often felt alone and abandoned. Something inside of me, for some reason, could not receive the love they had for me. I always struggled with feeling left out or less than others, not from anything they had done or not done, but from something inside of me. These young adults have had years and years of events that, honestly, give them the right to be so emotional. Opening our home and having them live with us and each other, has created a family that is strong and loving. Every year for the holidays, we open our doors to whoever would like to come. Often, we have kids who have been with us over the past years as well as other young people that some of our kids bring with them, knowing it is safe, and we will pour out our love on them. I always make sure to have a stash of extra Christmas presents for kids who show up, whether I know them or not. We also have a wall of fame with pictures of everyone who has lived with us through the years. The saying on the wall is "Family - A little bit of crazy, a little bit of loud, and a whole lot of Love." This is us. This is what you can expect in our home.

The strategy that has helped me when I am in the face of emotions is to not react in the moment. When accusations and names are being outwardly expressed with the intention of hurting you, take a step back. Choose to have the perspective that the individual does not mean this toward you, but toward others who have failed or hurt them in the past, you just happen to be with them in a moment of expressing their pain. Give the young adult a safe place to let their emotions out. Provide an environment that is not going to cause even more pain. If you were to engage in the moment, the likelihood is that you would cause more scars and pain because, you too would be lashing back at them, saying things you will later regret.

You need to find a way to express what you go through. Having a therapist or someone you can talk openly with, expressing the anger and hurt safely, is key. If you do not find this outlet, the likelihood is that you will build your emotions up and the time will come when facing a situation, you will not be able to keep yourself from reacting emotionally. Healthy outlets are important and set an example for young adults. When we responsibly work through them ourselves, they too will begin to do the same.

Another tool is to take the stance of not engaging when two or more individuals get into a disagreement with each other unless there is a concern about someone's safety. Give space for individuals to resolve their differences between them. Realize that the style by which you do so may be different for them. In my experience, young adults have made me aware that just because they raise their voices or speak to each other in a certain way, does not mean they are fighting. Often individuals are raised in an environment where this is normal for problem resolution, and we need to give them that place to handle their situations in a way they are comfortable while modeling different responses at the same time.

Decide to understand their perspective and let them work through things together but do not take sides when disagreements happen. They will try to get you to do so, but it is important to remain neutral, no matter what your stance is, to give them both support and security.

Discerning whether your engagement is necessary is important as they learn to resolve differences in healthier manners. You will soon notice that the arguments are less, and they do not get as heated or degrading. Setting the example and working through situations with them, modeling calmer behavior, helps them see and learn different ways to handle things. Be a model of how to handle disagreements safely and you will see change come.

Chapter 5
Love in the Face of Identity

To say we have had a mix of individuals in our home is an understatement. Helping them to find their own identity and freedom to be who they are and be able to hold their head up high is one thing that keeps me going. I love to see them overcome and learn to be free to be who they are. While some will not agree with me, it is about their choices, and I stand behind that. What they choose does not impact or affect me, it is for themselves, and I am called to love them, regardless.

The first two that come to my mind, as I start writing this chapter about identity, are Kearia and Tyler. As I told you before, Kearia and Tyler are siblings. They went through the same circumstances early in their life from living with their birth mother, maternal grandmother, birth father, and paternal grandmother. Each situation had its share of challenges but the results for Kearia versus Tyler are very different. Kearia is an outgoing, loving young lady who loves relationships and learning. She always has a stack of books wherever she goes and talks to numerous friends on her phone. She is social through and through. We often help her with placing boundaries, as she tends to get hurt because she wants to friend everybody who crosses her path. Tyler, on the other hand, is quiet and reserved. While he has friends for whom he cares, they are much fewer in quantity. He is content to be by himself, playing video games, reading his Bible, or looking at sports cards.

Both Kearia and Tyler have mental health challenges that are very different in form but true to who they are. Kearia's is an outward expression but one that has also caused her to depend on the creativity of her mind. One of the diagnoses she has is schizoaffective disorder, which means that she sees and hears things that are not there. Because of the issues and problems that she experienced with her family and peers; she created a community in her mind to help her feel like she belonged. It took me a while to realize that her responses were often to what was going on in her head and not in real life, especially at school. She has gotten much better at distinguishing between what is real and what is perceived, as she has opened up and developed healthy relationships that provide the security she was having to create in her head. It has been challenging, but we have stood by her side, not judged her, and helped her discover and become the beautiful young lady she is today. Kearia is extremely smart and is currently seeking employment as her next goal. I absolutely love seeing the victories that she had and will continue to have and look forward to what is ahead for her.

Tyler is much more inwardly focused. He harbors his emotions and thoughts internally, and it can be a challenge to get him to express himself or ask for things. Much of this comes from being berated when he would ask for anything when he was little. He could not ask for food or even toys, for fear he would be beaten. He takes comfort in things like cards and paper because that was how he created safety and comfort for himself when he could not have his needs satisfied. Recently, Tyler has started to open more emotionally, expressing his anger and discontent with certain things. Sometimes it feels like the years that have been bottled up are exploding and we must help him learn to channel and express things in a healthy and right way. He is growing and learning how to be the individual that he is while being challenged with diabetes as well as a cognitive delay. Helping him to realize the amazing young man that he is, regardless of these challenges is heartbreaking at times. But his resilience and perseverance have taught me so much. I value this young man immensely and know that he too will overcome, and we will stand in awe at what he accomplishes.

I also want to talk about Jodie. I introduced you to her earlier but have not shared a lot of her story. As I stated, Jodie came to me in a situation where she was separated from her two sons and had a hard time finding comfort in who she is. Over the past couple of years, this has changed. Looking back, I can see that often the circumstances she was facing were because she was trying to help everyone else around her and not valuing herself. Like me, she is a caretaker and gets lost in doing so.

One of the first decisions Jodie made, leading to her great transition, was to stop using drugs. As a mother, it is hard to watch our kids make decisions we want to rescue them from. But we must let them be and continue to love them through it, praying they get to the other side. Drugs were one of those areas for me with Jodie. Once she decided to break the habits, she admitted herself to rehab and has not turned back since. I visited her regularly while she was there as she had just given birth to my granddaughter Emmie. She needed unconditional support and love, and I gave her every ounce I could. Soon she was ready to try to move forward and back into her own home.

However, she still had unhealthy relationships around her. Relationships that continued to choose drugs and make other choices that were unhealthy for her and the two children she now had responsibility for, KJ and Emmie. While she loved the people in her life who were making these poor choices, she started to realize the instability it provided her and the kids, so she began putting up boundaries, such as not allowing certain behaviors in her home and refusing to let people take advantage of her as they had been. Watching her stand in these decisions and seeing the life that it has given her, and her children has been amazing. Today, I am watching her in a relationship that has provided balance, life, and love to all three of them in a way that Jodie is so worthy of. I am not sure where this relationship will go, but I am more optimistic about where she is and what is happening for her than I have been in a very long time.

Another young man who lived with me for a while is Damonte. This young man lost both of his parents at a young age and was separated from his siblings. He came to me, determined to make a difference in his life, committed to his education and building a career. Upon arriving, Damonte was enrolled in high school. Watching him push through to the completion of his diploma and take responsibility for every step was amazing. He faced challenges in some of his classes and with certain people but after talking with me and other adults, he would walk through and make the decisions to get to the other side, with grace and dignity. Do not get me wrong, it was not always easy, and he did not always make the right decision, but at each step, he took responsibility and continued to move forward.

Upon graduating from high school, he immediately enrolled in the community college. He also got his driver's license and purchased his very own first car. I can still remember taking him to the dealership and the smile on his face at his accomplishment. He loved that car because it was something he'd worked hard for, earned, and could say was his.

While in college, again he faced challenges with some of the classes. One class I think he ended up taking three times. Three times!!!! Can you imagine that? That is the determination and commitment he has. Currently, he is at a local university, getting ready to finish his Social Work degree. Damonte can honestly say that he is where he is today because of making the decisions, taking the steps, learning to stand on his own, and persevering along the way. This young man is going to be amazing at what he does because when he does something he puts his all into it.

Now I want to tell you a little more about Antony, who still lives with us. We met Antony through another young man who lived with us. Antony is transgender. While he was born female, he identifies as male. To be completely honest with you, I do not see a young woman when I look at him, I see a young man because that is what he has chosen. While this choice may not be in line with my personal beliefs, it is not my choice. My choice and responsibility are to love the individuals placed in my home, no matter what. Antony has lived a life of being condemned and devalued for his decisions, causing him to struggle with depression and more. It breaks my heart to watch young people be put down in such a way as this.

When he first came to our home, he was seeking the steps to make physical changes to his body, taking medications, and planning other physical changes to truly be who he is. While I never really talked with him about these in detail, I would listen and help him in ways that I could. I have noticed that he has discontinued the steps toward transition and has become more and more comfortable with who he is, not feeling like he has to continue to transform himself. He has a young lady who loves him dearly and they continue to work on and build life together.

For Christmas, last year, I remember I bought him a simple shirt, tie, and sweater that I thought would look good on him, and he loved it. You could see how much it meant to him that we would recognize this desire. So often people, when they gave him gifts, would get him girly things, trying to force him into something he was not comfortable with. I choose not to do that. Antony is an amazing young man who has a passion and desire to help and serve people. I look forward to watching him become comfortable and confident with who he is, while he achieves his dreams and goals. My love cannot take away the years of pain his heart has sustained, but it can help move him forward.

We have had a variety of individuals in our home, and I wish that I had time to talk in this chapter about every one of them. My love for them goes beyond what I can express, and I am proud of each individual and who they are becoming. Yes, there are a few who continue to make wrong choices, but I still stand here for them too. I continue to bear each one of them in my heart, hoping it is enough.

Identity is a personal decision. The tool I choose in these situations is, it is not about me. There comes a point in life where you must realize kids need to make decisions for themselves. While the decisions may not align with your values or beliefs, you need to back off and let them decide and walk out those decisions, supporting them while advising but not controlling them. I know and understand that this may cause heartache and pain, but they need to know someone is there, even in the times when things may not go as they planned or what they do does not align with your advice. Forcing individuals to do something because it is what you would choose often breaks your relationship or stops them from talking to you.

Young adults are at a place where they are discovering who they are and need the freedom to do so. Do not judge them for their thoughts or questions, as well as their decisions.

When they make decisions that do not align with your personal beliefs, realize that continuing to walk out as an example will make an impact as well. Quite often they already know that you do not agree with what they are doing but you, giving them the chance to explore and decide on their own, has more impact than you know. Trust and continue to support them, speaking your true thoughts without trying to control or manage the individual.

Yes, it often hurts to see them walk out their decisions but doing so without judgment makes it so they know they can come back when and if they try to make changes. If you fought with them in the front end of the decisions, the likelihood is they will not come back to you when they decide it was not a good decision. They do not want to be faced with "I told you so's" or "It was not my decision!" Keep an open line of communication and support for them.

Mental health is also a big aspect of this area. Often individuals deal with a variety of mental health issues, and they have been medicated, judged, rejected, hurt, and even abandoned because of them. These are not choices that individuals made, and they should not be made to feel like they were.

Learn to build upon the positive attributes of each individual, helping them to be confident in their strengths and passions. Every person is valuable and amazing inside, give them the chance to discover that within themselves. Decide to build upon the strengths of the individual and overlook the challenges – this will help quiet the voices the mental health causes and decrease the effect they have on them. Believe in them so they can believe in themselves.

Not all your young adults are going to go to college or be able to sustain a job. Some may not even have a high school education. Building upon their strengths and encouraging them will allow them to be who they feel and are confident in being. Yes, it takes time. Yes, it takes patience. But most importantly it takes an open mind.

Chapter 6
Love in the Face of Rejection

Do you know that in the United States, we put almost 25,000 kids on the street every year from foster care? That means 25,000 kids, every year, have not had a family they can depend on. These kids have been in the foster system and are now expected to navigate life on their own. They are often given their belongings in bags and sent out on their way. While things are getting better in this area with organizations trying to provide support services, often the kids do not want anything to do with them because they do not want to be a number, or they do want the freedom to make their own decisions and live their lives. I am sure you remember, being a teenager and wanting so badly to be an adult and on your own. I think that desire is ten times stronger for this population because they want the freedom they never had. For some, this was for a short time, but for many, it has been for their whole life.

I want to tell you about two people in my life, who mean so much to me. Jeffery and Kristine both spent their entire lives in foster care. They aged out of the system with no family, no support, nothing. I developed relationships with both of them over the years, making our way into each other's hearts to the point that we now call each other family.

I met Kristine through my son, Tyler. Kristine and Tyler played on a Miracle League baseball team together. Miracle League is a baseball league for individuals with special needs. I had heard through some of the athletes' parents, that Kristine needed some help with transportation to and from the games. My husband and I gladly offered to help and so began our relationship.

The first time we took her home she started talking about how she had been raised in foster care, causing her and I to immediately connect. I shared what I do, and she shared some of her experience. My heart was torn in pieces listening to her story, but more importantly, it was the beginning of a friendship that means so much to me. Honestly, she is one of the best friends I have ever had.

Kristine entered foster care at birth. I do not know why this happened, and honestly that is not what matters. The thing about Kristine is her amazing resilience and what she has accomplished in her life. Today, Kristine is in her 50's. While she is only three years younger than me, we have discussed guardianship and doing something official for her. It is not so she can call me mom, but more to have the knowledge that someone cares and is there for her if anything were to happen. The value of this goes beyond words for an individual who has spent their whole life feeling like they do not belong. I am ready and willing to provide this for Kristine.

You hear many stories about newborns in foster care and how so many families are waiting for a baby they can adopt. Unfortunately, not all end up as happily ever after. I have a friend who is a foster parent, and she uses the tagline "Foster Care, it is not all Unicorns and Rainbows." Well, it is not for the kids in it either.

While Kristine was adopted when she was a baby, the home she was in was abusive. She eventually landed back in the foster care system, never to be adopted or claimed by any family, but tossed from home to home for years. The number of homes she was in is too numerous to count. What kind of life is that? What are we doing to these kids?? I do not know the number of kids this happens to, but I promise you that we would be appalled if we did know. Many kids and young adults who have been in my home have experienced the same thing, being tossed from home to home. The effects of this are heartbreaking and we need to do something to change it.

Kristine did not let the circumstances of her childhood, which she had no control over, affect the trajectory of her life. After graduating high school, she quickly took the bull by the horns and entered the military. Look out Navy, here comes Kristine. She talks about her experiences in the Navy, how much she learned, and how strong it helped her become. Being in the military gave her opportunities to travel, see different parts of the world, and learn skills that she puts to use today. While she started in California, she ended up in North Carolina and currently works for the Special Olympics. She is a spokesperson for the organization as well as an ambassador at the US and World Games. She is amazing at speaking up for what she believes in and standing for and encouraging others.

When spending time with her and talking, I often wish I could just hug her and love away all the pain and trauma that the years brought her. Kristine has special needs, some caused by the trauma sustained and some from birth, but it has not stopped her. Nobody deserves to go through what she went through, but to say I am proud of her and how she has overcome the circumstances to create a life for herself is an understatement.

Jeffery is another young man in my life. Jeffery is my adopted son who currently lives in Texas with his wife Nicole, which, in and of itself, is an accomplishment. I first met Jeffery through the church when he was about 28 years old. Jeffery and his brother, Bill, were both in foster care. Bill was in a children's home while Jeffery was moved from home to home, sometimes even group homes, never landing in one place for an extended period of time.

When Bill was a teenager, he was adopted by a pastor and his wife, with whom he has an amazing relationship. I promised him I would use the words handsome and wealthy so here it is Bill with your name in the sentence. Bill is my pastor and has been for over nine years. He has a beautiful family with his wife and three kids. I am happy for how things turned out for Bill and proud of him and the dreams he is achieving by building a church community in our town. He is fortunate to have such amazing parents, and I know he knows that.

Jeffery, on the other hand, was not as fortunate. He did not have a family that claimed him, adoptive or otherwise. When I met him, he was struggling. He was homeless, suicidal, depressed, and alone. I had only talked to him in passing a couple of times but there was one day where he posted something on social media, and I could not keep myself from stepping in. He was communicating that he was suicidal and alone. I immediately called and talked to him. I called the police because of the situation and for Jeffery's safety. As I was talking to them, I got in my car and went to where he was staying.

Please do not be afraid to call the authorities when someone is expressing the desire to commit suicide. This is not the only time I have dealt with this, and I am sure that it will not be the last. The police are not going to arrest the person, but what they do is provide safety and someone who is trained to assess and support them. Sometimes individuals have been taken to the hospital for evaluation, but most of the time one of the officers who respond can talk with them and help them by listening.

Upon arrival to where Jeffery was, he was standing outside talking with the police officers. We went inside and I introduced myself and shared a little about what I do. I stood there, in front of the officers, talking about things with Jeffery and trying to encourage him to get help, explaining that I would be there to support him throughout. The officers agreed to let me take him to the hospital for assessment, which they usually do not do in these cases. As we drove to the crisis center, Jeffery tried to convince me to let him out of the car or take him someplace else, but I would not. We arrived and I sat with him until he was admitted. He stayed there for a few days, receiving the treatment and evaluations necessary to help support him. Upon discharge, he came and lived with us in our home to feel like he had a family there for him and to develop our relationship. As we spent the days together, our hearts grew closer and closer. I found out that he had been in the system since he was about 6 or 7 and he talked about all the homes he had been in. Again, my heart broke hearing him share his experiences and the effects that they still have on him today.

One day, Jeffery came home terribly upset. For most, it was a day that would have brought joy, but for him it brought pain. He had been at his brother's wedding. As we sat on the couch, he told me that the photographer asked if the family would stay in the sanctuary to have their pictures taken with the bride and groom. As you would expect, Jeffery stayed to participate and proudly stand with his brother. When the groom's family was asked to come forward, Jeffery started walking to the area. As he did so, someone looked at him and told him they did not mean him, just the adopted family. Rejection again, this time to the very core.

My husband and I, as well as his girlfriend at the time, sat crying along with him, feeling the pain that we thought he was feeling. How could I ever truly feel what he was feeling not being even close to going through what he was? At one point he came over and sat next to me, falling into my arms and weeping. As he did so, I looked at my husband and he immediately knew what I was thinking because we had a couple of conversations regarding Jeffery. I held Jeffery's head up and looked into his eyes and asked him "Can we be your parents?" His tears grew bigger as he fell into both of our arms and wept.

A few weeks later, we set out to get the paperwork done to officially adopt him but before we could get things done, he decided to go back to trucking. In so doing he met his, now wife, Nicole, and moved to Texas. Watching him settle down and create a stable life, alongside Nicole, has been an amazing testimony. Bill called me one day and thanked me for loving Jeffery. He was starting to see the changes and difference it made for him and was grateful to us and happy for Jeff.

The moment that Jim and I asked Jeffery to be our son really changed him. I am not glorifying what we did but what I am trying to express is the importance of belonging, the importance of family. Jeffery never had either. He never felt like he belonged and never had real family, a family that he could go home to on the holidays or even call him on his birthday. There was a void that was now filled that helped him settle and realize that yes, he was loved, and he belonged.

Can you just imagine how many young adults out of the 25,000 feel this way? They long to have a family or just to belong. Often it does not appear so because of how they act, but deep inside they do. Because they do not want to get hurt again, they put up walls, they act in ways that they think will make it so people will not love them, so they do not get hurt again. Sounds counterproductive, does not it? Well, it is. But if we can find people who are willing to commit and help them take down those walls, helping them feel like they belong and providing family, what a difference we can make. It only takes one person to believe in them, one person who is willing to stick with them through thick and thin as they work out life's decisions and build stability that they have never had. One person willing to love them.

I cannot begin to express how important belonging is, no matter what the age. While so many become accustomed to navigating life alone, there is always a longing deep inside to be part of a family, part of a community. Do not hesitate to make the commitment. I know that it is hard sometimes to commit to young adults, but they seriously need someone willing to do so, regardless of what they have put you through. Some of them will say they do not need you and even work their hardest to push you away but your choice to not back down and commit will go a long way.

Individuals who have aged out of foster care and have lived a life without any family still long to belong. They just need someone willing to commit to stand beside them, invite them for holidays, and even celebrate their birthdays with them. At this point, it is not about being their parent. It is about having someone next to them that they know they can depend on. It is about having someone there that will celebrate their victories and hug them through the challenging times. Make the commitment that you will stand beside them, no matter what. Yes, there are going to be times when you are going to want to run in the other direction, but that is true with any relationship. Choose to make the same commitment that you have made to birth children or other family members. You, deciding to commit, will change so much for them and you.

Chapter 7
Love in the Face of Loss

Not all foster kids are in care because of abuse and neglect, some end up in foster care because of losing their parents. I have had three young men in my home who have taken this journey. Each of them faced it differently as their circumstances and support systems varied.

First was Damonte who lost both of his parents in his teenage years. He has made the best of his circumstances and continues to thrive and move forward. He has a family friend in his life that he calls Mom, and she has been an amazing support to Damonte through the years. While I do not see or hear from Damonte much, I know it is because he is busy and focused on what he is doing. He is very dedicated and hard-working, even through the losses he has sustained.

The next young man is Nick. Nick lost both of his parents before reaching his teen years. He and his siblings were separated as well. Some were put in foster care, others had to navigate through life on their own because of their age. They did not have a family member able to take in all six of them, which is, unfortunately, pretty common. Nick and his younger brother were put into a home together. During their time there, they were both given the option of being adopted. Nick, since he was 16 or 17, at that time, did not choose this option. One of the big reasons he has shared with me that he did not, is that he did not want to dishonor his parents by doing so. What a burden to carry at such a young age. I am positive his parents would not see it as dishonoring, but it was the choice he made. Eventually, the family he was with decided to move to Virginia. At the time, Nick had 1 year of high school left and was not sure he wanted to move or change schools. It was during that time that I was contacted and asked if we had an open bed. We did and met Nick.

The decision was not an easy one for him to make at all. He was determined to graduate high school and weighed whether it would be better for him to finish in the school he already attended or move to Virginia and start over again, facing the possibility of differences in educational requirements and other changes. Nick chose to stay and eventually moved in with us. That was almost 5 years ago. He is currently working for a company he has been with for a while now and enjoying it. He and his siblings get together a few times each year and each of them is building their lives and families while still maintaining their sibling relationships. It is a beautiful thing to see but heart-wrenching at times as well. A couple of his sisters and his brother are currently expecting babies and I see social media posts they have wishing their parents were here to celebrate with them. They also talk about how they wish they were here to call and just get advice. While Nick has us to turn to, some of them do not have anybody who stepped into that role for them. I cannot imagine navigating through life and celebrating things like this without my parents when I was young. I tip my hat to them as they have all supported each other and been there with each other through thick and thin. I am proud of this family.

This subpopulation of young adults did not make these choices and are faced with the stamp of being a foster child in addition to the loss of their parents at a young age. Young adults who have been in the foster system are often misjudged and just trying to make the best out of life. I know that Nick will accomplish his dreams and that he, along with his siblings, will continue to build a life around each other and their kids. My love is not enough to bring back their parents or even come close to replacing what their parents meant to them or the relationships they had. Hopefully, it is enough, though, to give them hope for their futures.

Not all my crew has come directly through the foster care system, some have come to me later in their lives, like Jeffery. Another young man who came later in his life is Luis.

It was a Sunday afternoon and my husband and I were going out to lunch after church. My phone rang and my daughter, Jodie, was on the other end. Quickly getting to business, she explained that she was at work and asked if I could help her with something. I told her I would try and asked what it was. She continued to explain that she had a young man in the store that was stealing. She wanted to know if she could bring him to the house so I could help him. My husband, upon hearing the conversation, was not comfortable, in the least. He looked at me and stated that if he were stealing from the store, would not he steal from us? While I agreed with him, to a point, I continued the conversation with Jodie.

Jodie said she had gone over and talked to him and as she did, he began to cry, explaining that he had absolutely nobody. He was living in an abandoned house and was alone. I looked at my husband and asked if we could just give him a chance. We could have him come to the house and assess him. If we did not feel good, we could put him in a hotel for the night and then figure things out. He hesitantly agreed and I told Jodie to bring him over.

That afternoon Jodie and Luis arrived at our home. I quickly realized that he was strung out on drugs. As Luis and I sat on my front porch for a while and talked, he explained to me that he had lost both of his parents when he was young. Again, I do not know the specifics around their deaths but that is not what matters, he was without his parents since he was just a child. He proceeded to tell me that he went to live with his sister. She helped take care of him but once he turned 18, she required him to leave. Leave with no support, no plan, nothing. He tried to make things work by starting to become a plumber and he also had a relationship that was looking like they would be married. Eventually, things went south, and Luis got involved with the wrong people and started using drugs. The division began and eventually, his relationship with his girlfriend ended. Luis was able to hold on by himself for a while, but soon the drugs got the best of him. He started becoming more dependent on them. He lost his job, his house, his relationship, everything. As he sat there talking to me, he expressed that he was tired of the lifestyle he had built and he wanted to change, but he had nobody to support him. I looked at him and said that I would be there to help him with his changes. Assessing his situation, I informed him that, to have my support, the first thing he would have to do was go to rehab. I promised him that I would be there through every step and after, but that had to be his choice and first step. Luis agreed.

Not even a week before meeting Luis, I met a couple who live in my neighborhood and attend the same church we go to. When they came to our house, the husband looked at the wall of faces in my living room and looked at me, puzzled. I explained to him what I do, and he talked about how he loved helping this age group. He then stated that if we ever needed help, please let him and his wife know. I decided to take him up on this offer and called him. I fully explained the situation about Luis, explaining that he was homeless and informed them of his state. I asked if they would be willing to come and meet him. Once they did, they could decide if he could stay there for a night. After coming to our house and meeting him, they agreed and upon leaving, took him to Walmart to get some clothes and essentials.

That evening I called a few rehabs and finally got one where I was able to talk with someone in the intake area. After talking with them and hearing more about the program, I agreed to bring Luis the next day.

The next morning our friends brought him to the house, and he slept on the couch while I worked for a while. Eventually, I went and woke him, and we headed to the rehab.

On the way, Luis started asking me questions and in so doing recommitted his life to Jesus. As we continued our drive, he looked at me and stated that he could not remember my name but asked if I would mind if he just called me Mom. Tears trickled down my cheek as I said I would be honored if he did so. We then went and got some more things that he needed, including a bible, and headed to rehab.

Upon arrival, Luis was greeted by men who knew him. I looked at him in question and he stated that he'd been to this rehab before. I had no idea. The welcome helped bring him some peace but having Jim and me supporting him along the way helped bring the stability that he had been missing.

Luis graduated from the rehab program after 14 months. He has been committed, even through the challenges. Again, my mama's heart pride is overwhelmed with all that Luis has done and continues to do. To watch him walk in the humility that he has through all of this, committing and submitting to the leadership at the rehab including his counselors and sponsors, and making the decisions necessary to rebuild his life has been amazing.

So often drugs and other behaviors are used to fill a void. This young man had no support, nobody who believed in him. Now I believe that you must believe in yourself first to succeed, but that is for individuals who have had a stable environment with parents who love and support them. Sometimes, for this population, it just takes one person to believe in them. Luis did not choose to not have that support system; it was a consequence of tragic events that he faced. Once he had that support, he began to bloom and blossom. It has been beautiful to watch. I look forward to the years ahead with this young man, watching him grow, build a family, and live a life that is beyond his dreams. I believe in Luis, who can you believe in today?

It is not our responsibility or place to replace parents. Regardless of what individuals have been through, there is almost always a sense of loyalty and love. This is especially true for kids who have lost their parents. The circumstances that young adults, especially, face amid losing their parents are difficult to navigate. We should not force teenagers or young adults into adoption or any form of commitment that makes them feel as if they are dishonoring their loved ones.

Realize too, that there is often a fear in them that they may lose you too. While this may be unrealistic, it is a natural fear. There is nothing that you can do or say to give them comfort in this area as it is from the circumstances that were not planned, or intentional. They were events that took place that nobody had control over, and they are now having to navigate through.

Help the young person know and understand that you are there for them no matter what they decide. This is not about you and what title you hold but about them and providing them a sense of security and belonging.

The other important thing is giving them space to grieve when needed. Grief is not an overnight process and, for some may take years. Do not make them feel guilty when they want to talk about their parent(s). Encourage them to have pictures in their room or even put some up in your house, showing them that you support them as family. Often the kids feel like they have to forget their family to not dishonor you but help them realize that is not the case. You are there to celebrate and remember their parents and family and want to hear the stories and memories they have. This will not only help build your relationship but will also help the young adult with their grief. Knowing you care and seeing that the memory of their parents does not negatively affect you will give them stability. Be open and welcoming as you learn to embrace them and their memories.

Chapter 8
Love in the Face of Family Dynamics

It is weighing heavy on my heart today to write this. I intend to share a little, from the perspective of foster parents, regarding co-parenting and working with birth families. I will start by saying that family is real, family is strong, and it is never and will never be my intention to break up any family. At the same time, my responsibility as a foster parent, or parent period, is to protect the children and young adults in my care. I will do everything I can to provide a safe environment for every one of them, no matter what the cost is. It is hard, but this must be.

I started a state-wide organization to help provide support to foster parents and keep in touch with many foster parents and am active on the social media pages where discussions often happen. One of the questions often discussed is working through differences between birth families and what is best for the child. What is best for the child, so often gets lost because the adults are, not always intentionally, looking out for what is best for them, not the child. This goes for foster parents, birth parents, social workers, etc.

One experience I had was with my daughter, Priscilla. Priscilla was forced to go back to her father, in Arizona, after having no contact with him for over seven years. She expressed that she did not want to go. The plan all along had been for me to adopt her but, she was sent back to Arizona. It was definitely not in her best interest or safety to be returned to her father, but that is what happened, and my heart was completely broken, not once but twice.

Another experience is another young man I had for a while, Neil. Neil had been in foster care for a few years with a family that suddenly decided they did not want to adopt and had the kids that were in their home removed.

He came and lived with me because his siblings were with me at the time. While we were honest with each other about intentions throughout, one thing that was certain was that he did not want to be adopted by me, which was completely fine, and I supported him all the way. At one point we started taking him to families that were potential adoptive families so he could have a say in where he would go next and what family he would belong to. In the middle of the process, suddenly, the family that he had been with before changed their mind, after almost two years, and wanted to consider adopting him. The father came and met with Neil one-on-one. Soon team meetings with social workers, the parents, and myself were scheduled to discuss the transition.

As I stepped into the first meeting, I was extremely excited for Neil, as I knew that this was the perfect solution for him. He loved this family and always wanted to be with them. This was the best thing for him. The reason I am sharing this story is that, in that meeting, the social worker began to rake me through the coals as if she needed something to justify moving him. Why was the simple reason that this was what he wanted not good enough? Why did they have to make me sound so bad to complete this? To this day, I still do not understand all of what took place in that meeting, and I never will. I went in optimistic and willing to support this change with everything in me because it was what was best for Neil but left feeling defeated. I am not perfect and never claimed to be, but I love this boy and am so happy that he ended up getting what he so badly wanted. It is unfortunate that a system feels like they must put foster parents or birth parents down to accomplish their work, I have seen it happen both ways and it so grieves me when it is so unnecessary.

One of the strongest things for each person who has been in my care is the love that they continue to have for their family, regardless of the circumstances. I do have individuals that have no desire to continue a relationship with certain parents but, most of them still long to be loved by their birth families. Honestly, I even hate using the terms 'birth family,' 'birth mother,' etc. It seems so degrading to me and it should not be. I understand the need to distinguish between them, but I wish there were better titles to use.

I understand how hard it must be for a mother to hear her child call someone else Mom, but all of us need to be able to step back and consider the child, rather than what we want and prefer. The child needs a relationship upon which they can depend. Sometimes, being able to call someone Mom and/or Dad brings them stability and comfort. It is hard enough for them to be separated, especially when they do not understand or even know why. They are trying their best to get through what they are facing. If having caretakers around them that they feel they can call Mom and Dad is important, then we need to put aside our personal feelings to help and support them. It is not meant as disrespect to the natural parents at all. It is meant for the child. Many of us foster parents have tried to redirect kids in our care when they use mom or dad because of the dynamics of this very topic. But, again, it is for the child and how they feel, not us. I feel like I am ranting a little, but I want everyone to understand that it is about the child(ren).

Another lesson that I have learned is listening and holding my tongue. Not speaking, especially in any sort of negative way about the family, is critical. This is true even if I am just agreeing with the individual. The mix of emotions that the kids feel regarding their family is real and often they just need to get things out and talk about what happened or how they have felt. As their caretaker, I have found it best to just listen. Sometimes, even agreeing can get them into a defensive mode, as they want to protect their parents or family. They can become angry even though they are the ones doing the talking. The best thing to do in these situations is not to agree or disagree with them, but to validate their feelings.

For example, Tyler and Kearia often talk about their family. Even after more than 12 years, they still share stories, thoughts, emotions, bad dreams, and even good dreams that they have. As we talk, my intention is to help them with validating and expressing their emotions and how things are making them feel, not going into the specifics of the event or expressing what I think or feel about the situation. I remind them how much their family still loves them and how they miss them. I do not say anything negative or bad about their family, no matter what they have done or have not done.

Quite often this is a big challenge as a foster parent because we see and know things that the kids often do not know and should not know. It can be a hard line to navigate. For instance, I occasionally received notes and calls from a family member I chose not to tell my kids about. The calls were degrading and blaming me for the kids not being able to come back to them. That family member needed to vent and that was the form they chose. It is extremely hard not to take things like this personally, but it is my responsibility to put aside personal differences and continue to pursue what is best for the kids.

I have also opened my door to many parents over the years, by having them come for dinner, go to a park or an event together, and come for holidays. There are many opportunities to engage, encourage, and help to build and maintain relationships between parents and their kids. Some of these efforts have been successful and the families have been reunited, while some have helped young adults to rebuild their relationship with their parents, bridging years of separation. Young adults need to be able to do this on their own terms. Me, allowing them to bring their parents to my house, helps provide a place where they feel safe. They know I am there if needed, but honestly, I have never had to intercede in any way. I love to see their relationships restored or catch just a glimmer of hope of what can be.

It grieves me to see how families are often treated and the walls it puts up between them and their kids. Helping to bring those walls back down and teaching them to walk in forgiveness is important. There may still be dysfunction in the relationship but helping the young adults learn to put up boundaries for their safety and teaching them coping skills assists them to grow.

Sometimes, to protect the kids, I must make the hard decision of not allowing them to continue in a relationship, but that is to protect the kids. It is important to teach them how to handle certain situations and be able to protect themselves. Hopefully, in time, we can work toward restoring relationships when, together, we feel they are ready. Family dynamics are very sensitive and not easy, but they are such an important part of every person's life. Learning to navigate alongside them helps bring comfort and stability to them. Continuing to provide an environment and support to bring reunification is such an important aspect and I am committed to continuing to do so.

Family dynamics can be hard to navigate. The most important thing is the child/young adult. I know that your heart is for the youth, or you would not be here. Try your best to put your emotions aside and hear what the youth is saying through their words and actions. There are times we must stand in a hard place to protect the kids in our care and other times that we need to allow ourselves to embrace our emotions but not allow them to control the situation. We want every one of the kids to stay with us, as we feel that we are providing the best care for them but realize that the family is also feeling that way. Learn to look beyond the circumstances and situations that you may have a hard time seeing kids live in and understand how that child feels. While their situation may not be perfect or as good as you can provide, oftentimes, their parents love them and are doing the best they know how. Continue to be a support to the kids and their families, even after they leave. Knowing that you are there for them and supporting and not judging their parents helps in so many ways.

Understand what the family has been through. So often, the relationship the family has with you is based upon how they have been treated by the social worker or other people involved. We, the foster parents, are often the ones things are taken out on and we are the ones that find it hard to build a relationship with the parents. This too is not an easy road, as the parents have numerous walls up to protect themselves. They have been hurt and are constantly being put through the wringer with no support or love shown to them. The parents often need someone willing to listen and help them, rather than judge them. Do not get me wrong, this is not the case for some as there are some kids that we seriously need to protect. But, in my experience, more families need services and support to help them keep their families together, rather than tear them apart. Choose to face each situation with an open mind and heart, keeping the kids in the front.

Chapter 9
Love in the Face of Fear

Settling down is hard for some. Quite often it is due to the family dynamics in which they have lived. But I think they are often searching for something inside of them they desire and causes them fear, causing them to run away. These young people have so many fears; fear of being rejected again, fear of success, fear of love, fear of responsibility, fear of...I could go on and on.

Two of my boys, Dackoda and Coty, come to mind. As hard as it is to believe, Coty has been in my family for almost 10 years now. He came to me through a friend who helps homeless families. Let me share a story.

My Coty is an adventurer, which, in my opinion, is one reason he is such a wanderer. He cannot settle down. Coty had just started living with me. At the time, I just had Tyler and Coty, and the three of us went to spend a few days at Myrtle Beach. One evening, we decided to head to the boardwalk and pier area. Tyler had never been on a pier and wanted to see what it was like, Coty wanted to swim. As we got to the pier, Coty headed down toward the beach area, and Tyler and I headed to the pier. As Tyler and I stood at the end of the pier, watching the sunset and looking to see if we could see dolphins, a commotion started to build on the other side. One of the workers came running down and looked out over the pier, exclaiming, "Those kids will never make it back to shore, they are way too far out!" Immediately, 911 was called and everyone started looking over, watching the two boys.

As I looked out, I quickly realized that one of those boys was Coty. With my heart in my throat, I took off down to the beach area, explaining to the worker that one of those boys was with me. Soon you could hear the sirens and more people started gathering at the beach area. By the time the police arrived, Coty and his swimming partner were coming back to shore. The police stopped them and told them it was illegal to be swimming that far out. The young man with Coty started to argue with the police, causing one officer to tell him that if he did not stop, he would arrest them. I stood there hoping he would listen, but the young man continued to give the officer a hard time. Soon, the young man's parents arrived and got him to settle down. Fortunately, the officer let them go.

As Coty started coming towards me, a woman, standing next to me, looked at him and asked if he was with me. He stated that he was, and the lady told him he needed to give me a hug. I looked at her and exclaimed, "He does not even need to touch me right now!" and walked away. My emotions were a mix of anger and fear. Fear that this young man had just put his life in danger by swimming so far out and anger that he would do such a thing. We went up to the boardwalk and sat on a bench for at least 20 minutes until my heart stopped racing and I had calmed down. Once I got my wits about me, I looked at Coty and told him to never do anything like that to me again. To this day we often joke about this event and to this day he still pulls his tricks and shenanigans, all a part of his not being able to settle down.

Coty has not lived in our home for more than six years now, but he knows he always has a safe place to come visit or stay for a short period. I cannot begin to tell you how many places he has lived. Just in the last year, he has lived in at least six different places. I use the word places because oftentimes he is staying in a hotel, an abandoned home or shed, or even a friend's car.

Sometimes he gets angry at me and cuts me off, but eventually, he comes back because he knows I hold no grudges and that I will always be here. About two years ago he contacted me asking me to help him and his girlfriend, Mikayla. They came and stayed with us for a few weeks while we connected them with an organization that helps the homeless, which put them up in a hotel and helped him get a job. Through that job, he was able to get a house for himself and Mikayla, where they stayed for a few months.

While they were at my house, however, we found out that Mikayla was pregnant.

For the next few months, I helped them walk through the pregnancy and relationship challenges they had. To say it was a roller coaster is an understatement. Soon, their precious daughter was born, and everything seemed to be going well for them. About a month after their daughter's birth, Mikayla called me for help because the baby was sick, and she had not been able to sleep in two days. They had taken her to the local emergency room, but they were sent back home and told she had a cold.

I went down to their home to see how I could help and decided to bring Mikayla and the baby back to the house with me so I could help with the baby, and Mikayla could get some sleep. After the first night of them being with us, I noticed the baby was unable to keep any formula down, so we called her pediatrician, who told us to go to the emergency room. Upon arriving at the hospital, the nurses immediately put us in a room. When we entered the room, the doctor was already there waiting for us. A few minutes later the respiratory therapist came in and before we knew it, all kinds of emergency statements were made, and the room was swarmed with at least 15 medical personnel. Mikayla and I just stood there in shock. Our little girl had RSV and was in rough shape.

She stayed in the hospital for about a week and upon discharge, Mikayla's mother came and took all three of them to her home in Western North Carolina, about three hours from us.

Mikayla's mother tried so hard to be supportive of Coty and helped him with getting his driver's license, a small motorcycle to get him to a job, a stable home, and much more. Coty often butted heads with her because, as a man and father, he felt that he should be able to make decisions, but he also had to learn to balance that with living under her roof. Coty and Mikayla stayed in a couple of other places during that time but eventually landed back at her mom's. Again, Mom tried to be as supportive as possible and now, they found out Mikayla was pregnant again. Soon after learning of Mikayla's second pregnancy, Coty took off for Pennsylvania. Since then, he has moved back to North Carolina, living with various friends, family, and girls that he has met. The time he spent with Mikayla is probably the longest time he has spent with anyone. I was so hopeful that they were going to be able to build a stable life together, but he continues to wander. I pray for Coty often, that one day he will see his value, and that he will be able to break this cycle, the same cycle he lived with his mother. I honestly do not know whether that will happen or not.

I feel the inadequacy of my love to break this cycle for him, but I do know, that if he can truly find love for himself, there is greater potential for it to be broken. All I can do is continue to pray and support him, providing open arms and heart when he needs it. The rest, honestly, is up to him.

When I met Dackoda, he had just made the trek, on foot, from West Virginia to North Carolina. He contacted an organization that helped him before and they reached out to me, asking if we could help him. While we did not have room in the house, the individuals living with us at the time were adamant that we could not leave him on the street. We converted the dining room into a room for him to stay and moved him in. Crammed does not even come close to describing our house but the fact that individuals are willing to make the sacrifices to look out for each other speaks a lot about these young adults.

Dackoda was not with us long. He had a pregnant girlfriend he wanted to be with and support. She was close to having the baby and Dackoda asked if we would take him, so off to Georgia we went to meet her. Again, he is one of the kids that kind of go in and out of contact with me, and for a while, we did not hear from him. With Dackoda, it was usually because they did not have internet or stable housing. I would hear from him from time to time and everything seemed to be going pretty well.

I do not remember how long it had been, but eventually, I received a call that he was back in North Carolina. I made the hour-long trip to see him. We started rebuilding our relationship by spending time together and taking him to church with us. He had a really good job with a pool company and was trying to live with his father. Soon, things started to get hard in their relationship and he fled, I do not even remember where to. Currently, he lives in Western North Carolina and has been with a woman for over a year now. They just had my 9th grandbaby in December and are trying to build a life together.

Recently he called me, expressing interest in going into the military. This is not the first time he has talked about it, but it is the first time he has acted on it. I am hopeful that he can get in and that, through the military, he can start to build a stable life and environment for himself and his family. Dackoda has always struggled with stabilizing jobs and housing. I believe that he is afraid of success. He does not feel that he is worthy and gets scared in the middle of everything. If only he could overcome those things. As much as we love and encourage him, he needs to find the truth within himself. I think it would be good to separate himself for a while and evaluate what is important and what he wants to do. I am praying and wishing the best for this young man. He knows I will always be here to support him, no matter what or where he goes.

While these two boys are just an example of wanderers, many in my home wander from job to job. Mike, another young man who struggles with his value and worth, is a good example. After being told so many times that he would amount to nothing, he is a bad person, and frequently faced conflict that resulted in heated anger and emotions, no wonder he struggles. Being able to control and manage the challenges of these scars is a big task, but one that he has begun to face.

Mike is trying hard to discover himself and where he fits. He has tried numerous jobs from fast food to working in a gym to working for a trucking company washing the trucks. Unfortunately, Mike's anger sometimes gets the best of him. However, I am sometimes angry because of the amount of disrespect he gets in some work environments.

For instance, Mike worked in a fast-food restaurant in our town. One day one of the women called him Michael. He respectfully told her that he does not like to be called Michael and asked that she please call him Mike. This woman, mind you, was a woman who was old enough to be his mother, so she should know better, continued to call him Michael, often with an emphasis when she would address him. The first few times he continued to try to be respectful but eventually, it got to the point that he could not take it, so he quit. The fact that management knew about how this woman was treating him and did not step in for him, makes absolutely no sense to me. The good thing about the situation was that Mike did not get to the point of blowing up this time. There have been times I had to rush to Mike's place of employment because he was so heated and angry. One time the police were called because of it.

To say that Mike struggled in this area is an understatement. While most would not understand this, I have had to replace four doors in my house because of them being destroyed by him. While the events causing these actions have decreased due to Mike learning how to better handle his anger, the one thing I have told him is that I would much rather replace a door than have to pick him up from the police station or take an individual to the emergency room. While there have been times that his anger has been directed at me, there has never been an inkling of a threat or indication that he would do anything to me. He has gotten to the point now that he often seeks me out when he is in one of these stages because he knows I will help him talk through it, validating how he is feeling and helping him understand how he can better handle it.

The fast-food incident is not the only time Mike has been disrespected in the work environment which often causes him to give up. While I feel these experiences are important for his growth, I hope that he soon finds a job where he can connect with, someone who is willing to stick beside him and help him. There are not very many places willing to do this. On the flip side, many young adults have the mentality that the job is there to serve them not them serve the job, so they arrive when they feel like it and leave when they want, rather than committing to the schedule. While Mike is not one of these individuals, I do not understand this attitude. Still, I try to continue to support each one of them, helping them realize the responsibility they have for the companies they work for.

Wandering is big with this population, whether it be with housing or jobs. Helping them learn to love themselves and how to create a stable environment is challenging. All I can do is take one day at a time, helping them value themselves and realize their potential, negating all the naysayers. Hopefully, by loving them, and helping them love themselves, they will eventually be able to settle down and see their potential.

Fear is real for most of us. While most have fear of heights, fear of spiders, fear of, you name it, the fears that young adults face are usually unspoken and even unrealized by them. They are fears that are put up with walls of protection they do not even see or know about. Many of these fears are caused by years of experiences that have taught them to be on the lookout in a way they are not even aware of. Many have heard of fight or flight and that is exactly what is going on here.

Let's take Coty for instance. Coty, as I stated, is a wanderer. In the 10 years I have known him, he has not settled down for any length of time in any single place. It is constant change, whether it be where he is living or his job. There is something in him that fights internally when he starts to feel settled or comfortable in any way. This is caused by being in a constant state of transition when he was growing up. Again, this is purely my opinion, but knowing Coty and hearing about his life, I know that quite often he was uprooted and moved to different homes, whether it was with his mother or in foster care. He would get to the place he was comfortable and bam, they would move. This lifestyle has caused him to have a fear of success or of even settling. He keeps moving around and changing things because he does not want to be comfortable. It gives him control over his situation, rather than taking the chance that things will be good and help him settle, he would rather continue to make changes himself, eliminating the chance that things will again let him down, causing him to have to change.

Walking beside individuals who are constantly transitioning and unable to settle down can be hard and they can be the ones that try to push you away the hardest. This is due to the numerous people who have let them down before. They have learned that people do not really commit or stand by them through thick and thin, so they take matters into their own hands, continuously moving around.

Stand beside them, helping them but not enabling the behavior. I am usually pretty quick to provide support, whether it be financial or physical, but after a certain point, I discontinue doing so. They are still welcome, and I continue to be there for them but there must be boundaries. These are often hard. We want to take care of and provide the best for each one of them, but they must learn and navigate life.

Do not judge them but provide honest feedback and support. Help them see their gifts and provide encouragement. Individuals in these situations often call me to talk about things. When they do, it is usually everybody else's fault, and they are again a victim in their mind. Help them see what role they play and what they need to change, without condemning them or negating how they are feeling. Validating their emotions while providing them insight and direction will hopefully bring them to a place where they eventually settle. Some may never settle, and that too is okay. Allowing them to live the lifestyle they choose and being a support for them regardless is important. We want more, but ultimately it is not about us but about them.

Chapter 10
Love in the Face of Dreams

If I had my way, every one of the young adults that have come through my home would have their high school diploma, attend college or trade school, and work in a career. But things just do not work that way. Part of the issue is the reality of the system. Did you know that 45% of kids who age out of foster care do not have their high school diplomas? At least five of the young adults who have come through our home do not have their diplomas. Beyond earning their diploma, I want each of them to be able to find jobs that provide stability and for which they have a passion. Instead, too often they end up working in fast food, waitressing, or in jobs that pay minimum wage, making it very hard to be successful.

What does the word, success, even mean? Is it living in a big home with a career and salary, meeting the needs of those living with them while having extra? Is it being content living in an apartment or trailer where they are thriving and happy? I do not think one is better than the other. The best outcome is one where the individual and family are happy and living a full life together. With the occasional exception, it is common for individuals who come through foster care to continue the patterns in which they were raised. Our job is to teach them the skills to create independent stability for themselves and their families. Helping them realize they can build a successful life they are happy with, is the most important thing.

I do not judge if young adults need to use support, whether from the government, another agency, or from us. For instance, two of the young men moved out about the same time. Both of them were on a one-year housing voucher. At the end of that year, they lost their housing because no support was placed around them to help sustain it. The vouchers were provided by another organization, and they did not work with them to put together a plan. One was in school, and one was working a job that could not keep up with the amount of rent required without the voucher. This is a common and distressing problem. Both found themselves scrambling to figure out what to do. One ended up in another apartment with roommates for a little while and the other moved in with a family friend. This is not a successful transition. It is also not the failing of the young men. They are doing very well, are happy, and have, for the most part, created stability for themselves since then, but they should not have had to face the change the way they did. I did not bash them or the support they chose, I continued to encourage and help them so that they could navigate and work through the challenges in a way that was successful for them.

My dream for Jodie was for her to get her high school diploma, go to nursing school, and become a nurse, a desire she often expressed. We tried to get her GED and even tried her in a nursing program at the local community college. But life took hold. Currently, she is living in a town about an hour and a half from me with her two kids and her boyfriend and is expecting another baby. I wish she had not had to face so many challenges in her life, but they were her decisions to make, and I have stood beside her through each one of them.

It is not my responsibility to judge those decisions but to be truthful with her as she is making them. Once made, I stand beside her and watch her live it out, providing a shoulder to cry on when things do not go right and a voice to cheer her on and celebrate with her when they do. I still have dreams for her and want to see the best for her, but the best is based upon what she decides, not me. She is an amazing young woman who will go the extra mile for her friends and family. Now, she is learning to go that extra mile for herself. I want her to keep on dreaming because I know she can do whatever she sets her heart to.

Trayvon is another young man who has had a lot of challenges since moving out. I always hoped that Trayvon would go to school for something that would involve him working with people. While people are his biggest frustration, they are also his biggest passion. He has worked in daycare centers and grocery stores and always shows care for the people he is serving. He also chose to move out using the one-year housing voucher. After the year was up, he moved in with a family friend. Unfortunately, the situation ended tragically, and he moved in with other friends. The latest move he made was to Myrtle Beach to live with friends but now he is considering coming back to the area because his father has fallen ill, and he wants to be here to support him. While Trayvon has wandered with his living situation, he yearns for stability. His wandering is usually based on the needs of others. He often feels responsible for helping someone or satisfying an expectation they have, instead of following his own heart and dreams, and taking care of himself. I am hoping that one day soon he will be able to settle down and work on things for himself. While I understand the choices he has made to look out for others instead of taking care of himself, I also see the cost. We will be here to support him, however we can, when he moves back. We will let him make his decisions, advise him as he walks through them, and be there for the good and bad. Do not let the world get you down Trayvon – you got this!

I encourage you to support the young adults you know as they face the decisions that come with learning and finding their way. It is not always easy to watch them make decisions and learn to deal with the consequences, both positive and negative. The world they live in is so different from the way it was when I was their age. While some of the differences are bad, some are good, and we must learn together as they navigate through them. Encourage them to dream and dream big, but do not be discouraged if that dream looks different from yours. Our love is not enough. They need to learn to love themselves to accomplish things. They need to learn to put themselves first and believe in who they are. They need to be able to make mistakes and know that someone is there to support them when they do. Not someone who will pick it up and carry it forward for them but someone who will help them learn to stand tall and carry it forward themselves while cheering them along the way. Each person's measure of success is internal and one that we need to learn to celebrate. Today I celebrate the success that each of my kids has achieved, every single one of them.

Chapter 11
Love in the Face of Mistakes

Who among us does not long to feel "normal"? That longing is even stronger in young adults who have aged out of the system. Many were not allowed to even spend the night with a friend, due to restrictions. There are a lot of actions taking place right now to help fix these pitfalls of the system. Even if they were fixed, these kids will still walk through life with a magnifying glass on absolutely everything they do. Once they reach the age of 18, most do not want to continue to feel that way and will do everything they can to get out, can you blame them? I believe in rules for order and structure, but the reality is that the rules are multiplied 100-fold for foster kids as well as foster parents. Still, we all must work together to create an environment where young adults can navigate the world and be supported. This is important to provide stability and success.

Although many organizations provide services and support to this population, they often make the decisions for the young adults without asking for any input from them. Consequently, young people do not want to participate because they do not want to be told what to do or continue to live under the magnifying glass. These organizations have really good intentions, please do not hear me wrong on that, but we have several kids still falling through those cracks. Some kids do not even qualify for these programs. Sometimes, it is because of something they did, and other times it is because system requirements are not or were not being met. Most of these young adults just need someone who believes in them and will help them walk through the decisions of life.

When I spoke to one of my friends, who works for one of these organizations, she shared a conversation that had taken place that day. One of her young adults called her on the phone. As they were talking about therapy, the young lady asked if they could find a different therapist. My friend, with her supervisor listening, told her she would have to discuss this with the counselor that she was currently seeing within their organization. The individual wanted a therapist that better met her beliefs. My friend felt that, as a young adult, the client should be able to make that decision for herself and not be required to use one of the counselors there. I completely agree with this. How is this helping young adults to make decisions for themselves? How is this helping them discover what meets their needs? All my young adults have wanted this autonomy. They should not be forced to meet the requirements of a system. Something has got to change!

I would like to introduce you to Alex. Alex came to me when he was about 19. He spent the first year, after aging out of foster care, couch surfing. He decided it was time to change and he reached out to an organization asking for help. At the time, the organization would not provide services to him, but they knew me, so they called. We met Alex and allowed him to move in. One day, I was out and about doing errands and he came along with me. I had a meeting with someone at the local Department of Human Services. When Alex and I walked in, suddenly, we were swarmed by security. We were put in a room and required to stay there until the person I was meeting came down.

My appointment arrived and as she stepped into the room, she greeted Alex and asked what he was doing there. I explained that he was with me. She then proceeded to tell me that he was not allowed at this office. Not allowed at this office? Why? Alex and she then explained that an incident had happened where Alex posted something on social media, and it was deemed as a potential threat to one of their staff. I was floored 1 – that I was never told this and 2 – how can they tell a young adult that he or she cannot come to the one place that is supposed to be a safe place for them to get services? Trust me, I understand the risks that we put ourselves in, but we are supposed to be here to help these individuals. Later, I watched the video post that was deemed a threat and there was never anything directed at anybody. There were insinuations but more towards himself than their staff. This is one way that we do not provide normalcy, in my opinion. Labels are so quickly put on certain individuals, making success so much harder to reach. We did not force Alex to leave our home because of this. We did have a little higher level of awareness, but Alex was never a threat towards us or anybody else in our home. Alex continued to live with us and move forward as long as he was able. We continued to support and advocate for Alex as he continued moving forward, making several changes in his life. After he lived with us, his younger brother stayed with us for about a year as well. We were trying to help keep him out of the foster care system, which we successfully did.

It is a shame that so many young adults and kids in the foster care system think that they are going to be shipped out as soon as they make a mistake. This next story is one that I love to laugh at.

Nick had been with us for a few months and had been driving with my husband to get his driver's license. One day Nick had to go to work at Dairy Queen, so we let him use my husband's car. I had someplace to go that evening and decided to stop for some ice cream. Upon arrival, I noticed that Jim's car was not in the parking lot. I called Nick and he told me the manager asked him to run an errand and he would be right back. About an hour later, I again drove by Dairy Queen on my way home and naturally checked the parking lot. Lo and behold, our car was nowhere to be found. I got home, and once I realized he was not there either, I again called him and told him to come home now. Not in a mean or angry voice but one with authority. Upon arriving, Nick came into the room we were in. He quickly admitted that he had done wrong and apologized. I asked where he had been.

Nick had gone to Walmart before work and ran into a buddy. He was so excited to be driving the car that he and his buddy decided to go for a drive together. He stated how sorry he was and asked if he would need to leave. I said, "Absolutely not." We said that we understood the situation, but he should have given us a call and let us know his plans. I think most parents face this kind of situation. He did not do any damage to the car, nor did he do anything illegal, he just got hung up in the moment having some fun with a friend.

These kids should be able to make mistakes like this without having them documented in the records every time they do. Yes, they should have consequences, but they should not have to be drug through the mud for every little mistake they make. Nick's consequence was not being able to use the car by himself for a couple of weeks. They are going to live and learn, just like every one of us has done. I know I made my mistakes when I was that age, and my parents did not kick me out or disown me. Why do we do it to these individuals?

Normalcy is so important to provide healthy growth. I would like to see us take the magnifying glass off these young people. Yes, we need to help them attain certain standards but let's find a supportive way to do that.

Continue to stick with them through their mistakes. I can promise you that they are going to make some stupid ones. Unfortunately, the system is such that quite often they are removed as soon as they make a mistake or bad decision. This is not normal. We all make mistakes, and they need to be allowed to as well. Yes, some may hurt, but let it be an opportunity for growth for you and them.

Help them learn what alternatives they could have chosen, if any. The biggest role you can play is to help them by focusing on the positives. They have focused on the negatives and blamed themselves for everything, I promise you. They need to know it is not the end of the world and that good can come from it. Keep cheering them on.

You could be the ticket that keeps individuals out of jail. Sixty-five percent of kids that age out of foster care end up in prison or homeless shelters within their first year. Providing a stable loving environment will change the trajectory for some. Being willing to receive them in your home and love on them while providing them guidance and support is exactly what they need. We have had young men in our home who were part of gangs and chose to get out. Knowing they were involved was uneasy for us, but we do not regret the choice we made to stick by them. We made them aware that we knew and set boundaries and expectations but never judged them or their friends. This has impacted them and provided space for them to become stable and healthy in their relationships. Be a role model and you too will see lives change.

Chapter 12
Love in the Face of Death

This is the most difficult chapter to write. Just thinking about it, I have tears in my eyes. I am writing this on the 24th birthday of one of my boys. We lost him last year, last year was chocked full of loss for us. While the loss is not easy for anyone, there are some challenges that I have faced, as a foster parent, during times of loss that are just blatantly unfair and hurtful.

Losing a loved one is hard but losing a child is even harder. I introduced you to Priscilla earlier. She was and still is deep in the core of my heart. Quickly we had such an amazing network of people around her who loved her so much from my family, my church family, the school we had her in, and even a network of friends she had made over the years. She was the goofiest girl you would have ever met. My girls and I have memories and jokes to this day that we will text each other, like "Have you ever seen the arrow between the E and X in FedEx?", "You do not deserve to get me a straw!", "Did you see that thunder!", and "Chipmunk cheek truck", just to name a few. She would come up and lick you on the cheek to make you laugh or just give you one of her goofy looks. She was with me when my friend's baby, Sarah, was born and spent time with friends and family at the lake here in North Carolina and in Pennsylvania. Words cannot begin to express how much I miss her intelligent wit and the caring heart she had for others. She spent so much time talking to me about friends and the struggles just being a teenager brought them. Priscilla also loved photography and bringing out smiles in so many ways.

While Priscilla was with me, the plan was for me to adopt her right from the beginning. A couple of months into building a life together, we received a call that her father had contacted the social workers and he wanted to get

Priscilla and her sister, Hannah, back. Priscilla was devastated and expressed to the workers that she was not interested and wanted to stay with me. We tried to fight it together but soon she was moved. She and her sister had no say in the matter and were moved to Arizona to live with their father. There are so many dynamics around this situation that were wrong, but I choose not to digress.

After moving, I talked with Priscilla regularly, crying and comforting each other from a distance. At one point, her father cut off communication with me, because she was constantly telling him she wanted to come back. I had not heard from her in a couple of months when she messaged me asking to talk. She was at her lowest point yet and so unhappy with having to be there. She shared how she was struggling at home, and school and just not feeling like she was fitting in. I tried to encourage her, telling her she needed to give it some time. We talked about the possibility of her coming to visit me for the summer and discussed that we would have to work together to get her dad to agree. She got off the phone that evening a little lighter-hearted and optimistic, or so I thought. The next morning the call came, Priscilla had committed suicide and was gone.

I fell to the floor and screamed; my kids came running into my room to see what the matter was. I asked them to go get my next-door neighbor, Wendy. I could not move from the floor. Wendy came over and I told her what had happened and that we needed to tell the girls who lived with me. The rest is a blur.

I scheduled to go to Arizona for the funeral. Her father had agreed to have her kept so that I could see her one last time. As I stepped into the room to see her my heart completely sank. It was true. My Pri-Pri was gone at the age of 13. Never again would I get a lick on the cheek or a smile that lit up a room. Never again would I laugh until my stomach ached at the shenanigans of my little girl.

The funeral was a testament to who Priscilla was. Her sister, Hannah, and I went out shopping the day before and we got bright neon green and pink sneakers that we wore to the funeral. Other friends also wore her favorite colors or something that specifically reminded them of her. Friends shared memories and tears as we said goodbye to a bright light we would never see again. During the funeral, her father approached me and stated that he wanted me to take her ashes. What? Why should I take her ashes? "Because she always wanted to be with you and now, she can be", was his response. Internally that bit me to the very depth. Why would you wait until a time like this? Why would you not let her come back to me, where she belonged and wanted to be when she was alive? Why did you even have to come back into their lives after they had found loving families, and they had not heard from you in over 7 years? Why? Why? Why?

It is times like this that, as a foster parent, the treatment is so hard. I was honored to be treated like her mother at the funeral but the things that took place that were not seen or heard by most still hurt today. If you are reading this and you are a foster parent, I highly encourage you to make sure you have a strong support system that you can talk to. I know that there are certain things that we are not supposed to talk about but, trust me, you need an outlet and a safe place for those hard emotions. When children are removed from your care without any notice or even if you have been given notice, but are concerned for their "well-being", you will need support for those times when nobody seems to care or listen to you about your concern for the child/ren in your care and you need a place to vent, just like any parent would. It is for the losses and hardships that you will face that you never thought you would have to. It is imperative that you take care of yourself and know that you are not alone.

During my time in Arizona, I met some of Priscilla's friends, some of whom I keep in touch with today. I also keep in touch with her sister Hannah, who has grown into a young woman who continues to grieve not only her sister but the circumstances she was dealt with.

My little girl may be gone but every so often I get, what I call, kisses from her. These are little things that remind me of her and often put a smile on my face when I am having a hard day, or a laugh when I need to lighten up. My love was not enough to save her from death's sting, but it was enough to give her hope and life, if just for a little while.

My second loss is Alex. What a pistol he was! I met Alex when he was almost 19. He had been couch-surfing and realized he wanted more. There was very little that I knew about Alex when he moved in, all I needed to know was that he was a young man who wanted to make a difference in his life and needed support to do so. One of my favorite stories to tell is about Alex. I laugh every time I share this.

It was midnight, my husband and I were woken by the alarm going off in the van. We got up and went to the room of the young man who was supposed to have the keys and he informed us that Alex had taken them and the van. He had no license at the time and did not have permission to take the van, so I called the police and reported the van as stolen as he pulled off, with the alarms still blaring. As I stood on the front porch, waiting for the police, Alex walked up the street with his head held low. The only thing he said was that he was going to go pack his things. I stopped him and told him that it was not necessary.

At about that time, the police arrived, and we discussed the situation with them and Alex. We agreed not to press charges. We also told Alex that this was his one chance, if he did something like this again, we would press charges. I then asked where the van was, and he said it was down the street. As I began walking, I could hear the alarm still blaring. When I arrived, the back van doors were open as well. Once I got back home, he told me that he was trying to get the alarm to stop and was pushing buttons, which caused the doors to open, and he could not figure out how to close them either, so he walked away. He got so frustrated with trying to figure out how to get things to work, that he abandoned the van. I guess the lesson learned here is to have a van that has defective doors.

During his time with us, he continued to challenge us in some ways and had a temper on him, especially when things did not go his way. He often butted heads with other young adults in the house. At the same time, he was the first to offer someone help when they needed it. After an incident involving him and other young adults in our home caused his removal, we continued to love and support him, even after he moved out of the house.

Alex often cared for others more than he cared for himself. We currently have a couple of young adults living with us because of Alex. It was through the relationships that he had while in foster care that he brought friends who needed support, and some ended up moving in as well. As I have said, he was often looking out for other people, especially friends who needed help.

As he started to evaluate his future, he decided he wanted to become a paramedic. While in our home, we got Alex started at the local community college working with the coaching program they have for young adults who were in foster care. He started over a few times because he would be motivated in the beginning and quickly lose steam, start missing classes, and eventually drop out. The school staff were gracious and kept giving him chances and tried to coach him. I think one thing that you face with most individuals at this age is that they know everything. Alex was one of those individuals, to the core, and it was often hard to give him advice or direction.

Once he moved out on his own, he realized the importance of his education and started to settle down in his commitment. At first, he lived with friends or family but eventually, he got his own apartment, worked at least one job, went to school, and had a baby daughter. Alex also had his brother staying with him, trying to help him get on his feet and make better decisions than he did at his age. He was making huge strides and was proud of his accomplishments.

It was a Friday evening and I had been out running errands and helping some of my young adults in the community. I had stopped at a gas station to get gas and my phone rang. The person on the other end asked my name and once I told them, they simply stated, "I am sorry for your loss." I was confused and asked them what they were talking about, and the man apologized, thinking I had already been informed. It was then that he told me that Alex had passed away and I was the person he wanted them to contact.

Stunned is all I can remember, numb and stunned. He proceeded to tell me that Alex had been at a college graduation and had an asthma attack. He did not have an inhaler and the paramedics were unable to get to him in time. Just the day before, Alex and I had been talking about his daughter's 1st birthday party scheduled for the weekend. I remember how proud and excited he was about it.

I reached out to his family members that I knew and, fortunately, they had already been informed of his passing by Alex's girlfriend, who had been with him when he passed. I passed off the role that Alex had put me into on the family, so they were the ones to make the decisions. That evening, I went home and fell into the arms of my kids as I told them that Alex had passed. While there was often contention and strife between Alex and the others, they were heartbroken over the news. To be honest, we did not talk about it much and I realize now that some of that is because they were having a harder time than I thought. On the day of the funeral, only one of them was even able to attend.

I spoke at his funeral and some of what I said I regret because I did not know his family was unaware of some of the circumstances that Alex had faced and overcome. My message was that of unconditional love and forgiveness, two things Alex started to be able to receive and walk in. Alex could sometimes be a troublemaker, but he had such a way of making you mad at him one moment and within a matter of seconds want to hug him. Through it all, we never gave up on him. Even when he had to leave the home, we still welcomed and supported him as much as possible. Being in the system, he was used to people turning their backs on him over the smallest things and eventually those small things became big. I am proud of how he started turning things around, extending forgiveness to himself and others. I watched him restore relationships with family members and exercise patience as he did so. All the steps he was taking and the difference he was making for his life as well as for his daughter were beautiful to watch.

The big challenge for me in this loss was the perception other people had regarding how I should not be grieving since he was 'just a foster son.' While I may not have birthed this young man out of my body, I put all my heart and soul into him all the days that I knew him. No, he was not bone of my bone or flesh of my flesh, but he was a young man in whom I invested, even if it was for a short time. Please understand that, as foster parents, we love every child, young adult, kid, and person, who comes into our home like they are our own. Yes, we respect the fact that most of them still have family that love and care for them, but we do too. I am not just a foster mother, I am a woman who loves every life put before me unconditionally, which means that when I face loss such as this it hurts. While I cannot tell you what it feels like to lose a child I have birthed, I can tell you what it feels like to lose one whom I love deeply. It hurts and it hurts bad.

We miss him so much, as do the young adults in our home. He was an extraordinary young man with great potential and his life was taken way too soon. I often wonder why some die so young. I will never know the answer to this question, as none of us will. What I do know, is that Alex will always have a special place in my heart. Was my love enough for him? It was not enough to keep him here but hopefully it was enough to bring healing to himself and others.

Both losses have left holes in my heart. I stated the importance of having support systems around you that believe in what you are doing and can lend an ear or shoulder. Loss is hard but loss with the lack of support is even harder. Lean on those who support you without judging or shunning you or the kids. My mindset is always to stay strong. I push myself through these types of situations and then suddenly, I crash. That is not healthy. Make sure that you are taking care of yourself. Find a way to express and get out the things you need to, it will provide a much healthier life and mindset for you and the kids you serve.

I hope that you never have to face the death of a child. If you do, do not let others tell you how you should or should not be grieving. Grief is personal and is felt and expressed differently for each of us. As a foster parent, your heart is vested in every child/young adult that comes through your door. No matter the amount of time or situation, we care, and we care deeply. You have every right to feel and express your loss. Take care of yourself and permit yourself to grieve.

Do not give up either. I know it is what I wanted to do both times, but I did not. Realize the difference you made in the kid's life and the difference you will continue to make for others. With that said, it is important to know and understand the space you need to give yourself at the same time. If you need a break, take it. If you need to talk, find someone with whom you can. Be aware of your needs and fill them. You must be filled back up before you can continue to pour out to others.

Death is hard and never gets easy. Knowing the circumstances behind them can also cause us anxiety and a list of I should haves or should not haves. Do not let yourself get taken by them. You made the decision or supported the decision that was made the best you knew how to. Circumstances did not end up in a way that you would have liked but it is not your fault. There is nothing that you could or should have done differently. Trust in the time that you had and know that you made a difference. Know that you continue to do so.

Chapter 13
Love in the Face of Grief

I know that this is not the happiest part of the book, but it is important to think about before it happens. Many of us, as foster parents, have faced grief and supported young adults through the journey. I have already expressed the importance of supporting individuals in our care regarding their relationships with their families. Walking through a time of loss with young adults brings another level of intensity, as well as an opportunity to extend unconditional love.

The first loss we faced was Jodie's mother. Unfortunately, she chose a life of addiction that caused major medical problems. She struggled for a few years, going in and out of the hospital, in touch with Jodie one moment and absent the next. Jodie would often call me when her heart was breaking to talk about the emotional roller coaster she was on. Through the years I comforted and supported her, sometimes taking her to visit her mom in the hospital or doing whatever she needed.

When Jodie's mom eventually passed, Jodie was torn. I was there to support Jodie at the funeral and after. I know that Jodie misses her mom. I know that there is nothing like losing a mother, and I will continue to be here to listen and support Jodie as she continues to move forward with her life. It is important, in situations like this, to put aside any opinions we may have about the choices someone makes and love and support the individual in our care. It means so much to them and speaks abundantly to the young adult regarding our respect and care for them.

The next loss was when Aech lost her mother less than a year after moving in with us. She and her two sisters faced the hardest situation I have ever watched regarding the loss of a mom. Even though they did not live with her, and they had been physically separated, they were emotionally close, talking together regularly. These girls loved their mother and deserved to be included in the decisions.

Their mother was in a relationship and her partner made all the decisions and ran everything as if he were the only one concerned. The girls were not shown the respect or given the honor they should have been given as her daughters, which caused their grieving to be even more difficult. I find it disgusting how so many people think that someone who has been in foster care and lost their mother or father would not grieve over that loss. I have learned that no matter what a parent has done to a child, the likelihood is that that child/young person, will always love their parents. Now, do not get me wrong, there are definitely some- circumstances for which this is not true, but in my experience, the kids still love their parents, so when loss comes, it comes hard because oftentimes they have spent years separated from them. Even kids who have chosen to not forgive their parent(s) grieve hard, sometimes even harder because there was never any resolution between them. Aech and her sisters had a good relationship with their mother, and I love hearing stories about her and how each of them is like her in different ways. I never met their mother, but I still grieve her loss for the girls.

This past year, Coty and his sister Alex, yes, another Alex, lost their mother. Like I said before, Coty has been in my life for 10 years, so I had a lot of life lived with this family. Alex was never in my care, but we knew each other enough that she knew she could call on me. I had seen posts on social media that Sharon, their mom, was in the hospital again.

Their mother, Sharon, had been in and out of the hospital numerous times over the past few years but this time was different. Alex was informed that their mother had an advanced stage of cancer and there was nothing further they could do. At the time, Coty lived a couple of hours away and he had not been talking to me, but I called him to see if I could get him to come to the hospital. I told Coty what I knew and scheduled a time to go get him. On our drive, Coty expressed how he still was not on good terms with his mom and expressed his discontent with everything. I simply listened.

Once we got there, the doctor wanted to speak to us. She informed us that the cancer was affecting Sharon's organs and they had to make a decision. She shared what options were available, then Alex, Coty, and I went to a private room to talk. As I sat there listening and asking them questions to help them make their decision, I knew I had to keep my emotions controlled. They soon decided to discontinue any support that their mother was getting and let her go. We then sat back for almost a week watching her fade further and further away.

I provided support for them by taking care of Alex's son, planning arrangements for her with a funeral home, as well as holding a memorial service for friends and family. To this day, Alex continues to grieve for her mother. She was her source of support emotionally, physically, and mentally. Being with her through this time has changed my relationship with her. I am so proud of this young woman and the changes I see her making for herself and her kids. As for Coty, my heart breaks in pieces as he continues to wander from place to place, finding no stability. He always knows that I am here for him and that I love him, but for him, my love has not been enough. It has not been enough to help him out of the trenches and years of destruction. All I can do is pray and continue to be here for him along the way, speaking truth in love and supporting him.

There is nothing like losing a mother. I can say this from experience as I lost my mother four years ago. I miss her terribly and often wish I could pick up the phone and call her or just hear her voice one more time, but I rest in peace knowing she is in a much better place. When young adults face the loss of their mother, there is often a mix of emotions because of what they have been through. I would be concerned if they did not have that mix. The most important thing, and I know I have expressed this a few times, is that we support the young adult with where they are at. Please do not tell them how they should feel or express anything negative about their parent, no matter what the circumstances are. Providing unconditional support and love for them through this time means a lot. Trust me, they will often try extra hard after this to push you away even more. Again, that stems from two things. One – They do not want to get hurt again or Two - They do not want to dishonor their parent. Stand beside them with no expectations and simply love them. Sometimes it will not feel like enough, but it will be in the long run.

I know that I will never replace their mothers. I have no intention of doing so for any young adult that has been in my care. Even if the child-parent relationship was not the best, it is not my place to put them down or try to be better than they were. My place is to be who I am in their life, extend love where they are, and support them while honoring their parent for their place in their life.

When a young adult experiences the loss of a parent the best tool you can have is to be there for them. You should have no expectations or opinions regarding what they are facing unless they directly ask you and even then, do so with wisdom. Do not express any dishonor to their parent, regardless of the circumstances around their death or their relationship. The young adult is going to be sensitive about these things and you need to show them as much positivity and support as you can. Nothing of what they are facing is about you.

This is a time when words may fly, trying to push you away. Do not take anything personally. Help them process their emotions and be supportive of them and what they are going through. For many, you are all they have left.

Another lesson I learned was that of being a support for them when dealing with funeral homes, hospitals, and other systems. I was shocked at the way that Alex and Coty were treated when they lost their mother. We went to a funeral home to make plans and they did not even express condolences or anything to them but immediately expressed that they would not do anything for them until they received payment, completely contrary to what they told us on the phone. We walked out of that funeral home in complete tears. I was so glad that I was there for Alex and Coty as they would not have handled things well if I had not been there. I honestly wanted to openly express discontent, to say the least, but it was about them, not me and I needed to keep the peace.

It is hard facing loss and the judgment and lack of support that often comes when it happens can make it even more difficult. Losing a parent creates such a roller coaster of emotions and feelings and at this stage of life, they often react to those emotions rather than logically. Be a support and advocate for the kids while teaching them how to respond to organizations that do not handle things the way they should. Nobody should have to face these circumstances at the time of losing a loved one, but unfortunately, it happens.

Most importantly, be a strength for them. Be there as a sounding board and resource they can depend on. Do not express opinions but allow yourself to grieve with them. Doing so shows them you care.

Grief is never easy and often comes in layers. Most are not going to face all the stages early but may take years to work through. Allow them to work through things in their own time and way, continuing to be a support and not judge them for it. It may look ugly at times but that is okay. They will get through it and so will you.

Chapter 14
Love in the Face of Determination

The walls that these young people put around themselves are real. There are walls of hatred, walls of abandonment, walls of rejection, walls of judgment, walls of anger, walls of strife, walls of chaos, walls of bitterness... I could go on and on. Over the last few years, I have faced a lot of these walls as the hurt and pain felt by the young person has been taken out on us. When you take the time to look at what these young adults have been through, it is easier to understand why they come across as cold and unfriendly. It is not a choice; it is a result of events in their lives that have caused these walls to be erected.

I have talked a lot about the walls that bring strife and challenges, but I want to talk about the power of healthy walls. These are walls put up by individuals that help them continue, in the face of adverse circumstances, to build personal success.

Drake's walls were that of determination. This young lady was determined to make a difference in her life and overcome every obstacle that she faced. Drake never lived in my home; she was living with her brother when I met her. I watched her push herself through high school. I stood beside her, helping her with changes she needed to make regarding what school she was attending and deciding on what courses to take, helping her make her own decisions at a very young age. Attending events throughout her high school years, participating, and learning what her passions were. I loved watching her grow.

We celebrated her graduation with a party held at a local park for her friends and family and quickly watched her charge off to a local university. I remember helping her move into her first dorm. It was so ridiculously hot because the air conditioner was broken in the dorm. We had to walk up and down steps with all her belongings. What a memory that is. Through her college experience, she participated in different organizations that helped her build her support network. One program gave her opportunities to travel and participate in summer internships, preparing her for her career. These experiences also allowed her to build relationships that would provide her with opportunities once she graduated. Upon her college graduation, we helped her move to Texas, where she is currently employed by a major corporation and thriving.

Drake's determination and independence have always stood out to me. Even without the support structure many others have, she has accomplished so much. Yes, she would call and lean on me from time to time but everything she has done she has done for and by herself. Even when she was in high school, I would often say, "Remember me when you get to the top." And, I have no doubt she will do just that, get to the top. By using her wall of determination, she has made a difference for herself while helping her siblings realize that they too can thrive.

Alexis, who lived with us for less than two years, also has that wall of determination. One of my favorite memories with Alexis is when she and I went to Wine and Design together. We were painting owls with ladies from our church sharing lots of laughs and having so much fun. One thing you should know about me is I can get playful. One way of doing so while painting is to 'slip' and get paint on friends around me. Alexis was my primary target, or should I say victim, this evening.

As we continued painting, Alexis looked over at me and simply asked, "Can I call you Mom?" My heart burst as I embraced her, confirming her request. Moments like this are forever cherished in my heart and Alexis claimed her forever in that moment. It does not take a day in court or a piece of paper to commence these moments, it takes two hearts. Two hearts that have connected and committed to walk through life together, through the good and the bad.

When Alexis came, she had some goals and was determined to make a difference for herself. She quickly registered for the local community college and attended until she had to discontinue due to her pregnancy. She then got a job and worked responsibly, while taking care of herself throughout her pregnancy.

While pregnant, she wanted to create a home for herself and the baby. She still lived with us when her baby girl was born but after a few months, she had saved up enough money and worked with an organization to get her own apartment. Since then, she has worked and attended some classes and is now trying to start her own business. She has faced the world with tenacity and determination that is making a difference for her and her daughter.

These two young women are making a difference in their lives and have done so in a healthy way. That does not mean that they have not made their mistakes or been without challenges along the way, but their determination outweighed each of those and helped them get where they are today. Sometimes those walls of determination came with a bit of pride that prevented hearing suggestions, but I would speak and let the rest be up to them.

I shared Damonte's story earlier. He too, had the determination to move forward and accomplish his dreams. While, for some, those dreams have changed, it is a journey they have been allowed to live and make decisions through.

This brings me to my next tool. Believe in them. I have said it a few times how we need to allow each of them to make their own decisions and believing in them is part of that. Unfortunately, most of this population have not been able to think about or dream for themselves. They are often told what they can, cannot, and should do. Give them the space to discover for themselves, encouraging them along the way. Provide opportunities for them to explore different things, opening them up to a new world of possibilities. Dream big with them. Many states pay for a college education for young adults who have been in the foster care system, even if they did not age out of it. Help connect them with resources to do so, whether it be community college, trade school, university, or another form of education. There are usually other organizations that provide support and resources to them as well that you should familiarize yourself with. Provide them with information to connect and let them do so. Do not force them to do any of it but give them options, help them understand the options, and be willing to talk about them over and over because often they do not remember.

As you believe in them, remain flexible as they are bound to change their mind multiple times. Do not judge or scorn them, coach and encourage them. The more positive you are the more positive they will become and eventually something will stick. Even individuals with determination will hit walls and change their minds. Encouraging them is going to be important because oftentimes it is discouraging to them when plans do not go as they had hoped. Help them understand that it is okay and help navigate them through their thoughts and feelings. You are a sounding board and anchor for them during this time. Stand firm by giving feedback and advice but not setting expectations. Let them set those.

You play a very important role during this time of discovery as not only are they discovering themselves, but they are also often discovering how to create a positive support system. Open them up to possibilities and be there when people fail them. Be their rock!

Chapter 15
Dear Police Officers

I cannot even begin to tell you how many times police officers have been to our house. Most of the time it is due to an argument that has turned into a physical altercation or a neighbor calling the police after hearing the arguing. We often joke about being on a first-name basis with some of the officers. While I truly appreciate the police officers, there is a need for more awareness and training when responding to situations involving someone who is having a mental health issue. There is a difference.

Criminal incidents and those involving mental health issues are different and need different responses. There are times when individuals with mental health become dysregulated. Their emotions get the best of them, and they act out in a way that is not in the best interest of themselves or others. While police may be needed to bring a level of authority, safety, and peace to the situation, sometimes they use that authority in a way that escalates the situation and may cause things to get worse.

Most of the events that we had were handled pretty well but there have been some instances where the police have made the circumstances far worse and not helped the situation at all. One incident resulted in two of our young adults being arrested, which should have never happened.

One night Jim and I were woken up by Antony and Aech arguing, unfortunately, this was not uncommon. This evening, however, they were really upset with each other. At one point the two of them went outside. One of them began chasing the other down the street, the two of them screaming at each other. It was after midnight, so we urgently wanted to get things under control to not disturb the neighbors.

We got the two of them to come back inside and sat them both down. They settled down quickly as we sat on the couch discussing what was going on, trying to help them resolve it without the drama. About 15 minutes later there was a knock on the door. I opened it to see three police officers standing at the door. They asked if everything was ok and I stated that yes, it was, and we had the situation under control. They asked if they could come in and insisted on talking to Aech and Antony.

One of the officers demanded that Antony step outside so they could talk to him. Before we knew it, things had blown up again. We heard raised voices outside so Jim, Aech, and I walked outside to find Antony in the police car kicking at the windows and hollering. Aech went over to talk to the police officers and before I knew it, they had decided to arrest her as well. I still do not know and understand why as she was simply talking to them and complying with their requests. She was not speaking to them disrespectfully or causing any additional trouble. She just started walking towards me. Suddenly, they demanded she come back and walked towards her, grabbing her by the arm, stating she was under arrest. They put each of them in separate cars and off they went.

Antony and Aech have been dealing with court and probation officers ever since. While this situation is coming to an end and I am proud of how they have handled it and the changes they have made, I am still so grieved by how it was handled that night.

I also shake my head, sometimes, at the judicial system. Aech and Antony have been in court for this more times than I can even count. Most times, the case is continued, completely wasting their time as well as their attorneys' time. This aspect of the judicial system confuses me. Sometimes I feel that the judicial system has treated the young adults in our home worse than a person who held up a bank at gunpoint or even murdered someone. The treatment and the runarounds they were given and the seeming efforts to make them feel 'less than' did not result in good. It produced stress. Is that truly what our system should be doing? I do not write this to put the judicial system, down but I do think changes are needed to many of our systems. We need changes that lead to more positive outcomes.

Another incident I had was with my daughter, Kearia, who was living in an adult group home. Due to her diagnosis, she sometimes needs to be admitted for mental health needs. This event occurred during one of those times. I had gone to the magistrate's office to complete the paperwork. She was having some behavior issues that were concerning to myself and the staff and we needed to get her admitted for some evaluations. After obtaining the paperwork, I went, picked her up, and then called the police, asking that they meet me at the hospital. To have her involuntarily committed, police were required to bring her to the hospital. The police usually come to get the individual, but I asked them to let me bring her to protect and help her through the process, to which they agreed.

Upon arrival at the hospital, Kearia was in a minor state of crisis. She was very unhappy and was having some issues handling her behavior. We met the police officer at the doors and were immediately taken back to a room off the emergency room. Once in the room, Kearia started to give the nursing staff a little bit of a hard time while they were attempting to get her vitals. At one point, the police officer got extremely authoritative and started threatening Kearia, telling her if she did not cooperate, he was going to cuff her to the bed. The nurse and I looked at each other in complete shock. The nurse looked at the officer and asked if he could stand outside the door. Once we got Kearia settled, I asked the officer if I could speak to him in the hall. He was a young gentleman and I spoke to him about how he had handled the situation, explaining that for individuals in this type of crisis, the last thing they need is someone trying to exude authority and threaten them. It is oftentimes experiences like this that cause them to act and react the way she was. I encouraged him to learn to handle these situations with more compassion and understanding. His role should be to help settle the situation, not make it worse. He asked me a few questions and thanked me for talking to him.

I want to give police officers and other individuals who may respond to someone who is acting out due to a mental health or emotional crisis a message. Sometimes, an understanding ear and a calming influence will work far better than a strong show of authority. While I know it can be hard to immediately assess whether someone is in a mental health state, I ask that you please take a moment before acting. While your authority is often needed to help provide safety to others, it does not always need to be exhibited to the individual in crisis. The individual in crisis needs someone to listen, watch, and try to understand what is going on.

While Kearia's situation ended up fine for her, Aech and Antony's did not. Please understand, that these individuals are not trying or intending to cause trouble, they are hurt and broken and just need your help. Your support and understanding through their event could change so much for them. Choose to be a positive influence and help them. You make a difference, whatever your choice may be.

Chapter 16
Dear Neighbors and Community

Most of my neighbors, friends, church family, and community have been absolutely fantastic and supported me in helping these kids. Some of them took a little work to get to that place. Others wanted absolutely nothing to do with the young people, especially young adults, and gave them a hard time in so many ways. It is heartbreaking how so many people judge this population simply because they know they have been in foster care. It blows my mind that people blame and shun the kids just because of this fact but unfortunately, it happens, and it happens frequently.

In my first home, especially when I was fostering younger kids, I had neighbors who were always there for me. They helped provide meals when we had illnesses, watched the kids for me, welcomed them to play with their kids, and so much more. My church community, at the time, was also very welcoming of the younger kids, always wanting to hold the babies when they were around and helping with meals as well. It was not until I started taking care of the teens that things started to change.

The neighbors we had continued to welcome and help in any way they could but, unfortunately, things at church started to change a little. A situation with Kearia appeared to be the defining incident for the change. As I stated, Kearia could sometimes have events that became rather uncomfortable for some. Quite often these events would occur when she was triggered by something socially, like someone ignoring her or her thinking someone was saying something about her. Because of a couple of events, I was soon contacted and told that not only could Kearia no longer attend the youth group, but no more kids in my home would be allowed. When I asked why that decision was made, I was told they did not know where these kids came from and did not want them around their own children. What kind of a testimony is that? Are not we called to love the unlovable? Are not we called to take care of the orphans? This, along with other things, caused us to eventually leave and find a place where the kids were welcomed and allowed to participate.

Eventually, we moved homes, bringing with it new neighbors and challenges. One of my boys wanted to become a fireman and the town next to us had a program where members of the volunteer fire department had the opportunity to have their education to become a fully qualified fireman paid for. We moved into a tiny little 1200 square foot house with me and, at the time, four boys. By the time we moved out, I think we had six. Now I wonder how in the world we did it.

While in this home we had two neighbors that presented some challenges. We ended up being really good friends with one and the other was this way with absolutely everybody in the neighborhood. Our new friend lived across the street from us. He was an older, retired gentleman and would often sit in the window looking over at our house, or seemingly doing so. Once my kids expressed concern, I went over to talk to him and his wife to get to know them. They ended up being a great support to me and the kids, giving rides and sometimes someone we would just sit and talk with. We got to the point that when we saw him, we called him the nosy old neighbor. He would laugh every time.

We have had incidents in two different neighborhoods where someone called the police because the young adults were sitting in their car. In the first incident, the kids were in the car talking because there was no privacy in the little house we were in. They decided to have a conversation in the car, and someone called the police. Why??? They did not have any music blaring and were not doing anything they were not supposed to, they were just talking. The other incident, however, involved music, just music. A few of the girls were in their car listening to music. They were having a hard time because it was their mother's birthday. She had passed just six months prior. This was their way to grieve together. Although they were not doing anything they should not be, someone felt the music was too loud and called the police.

Another event involved Mike. One afternoon, Mike was having a hard time with something. He decided to go out for a walk, and he had on his headphones. Have you ever sung with your headphones on? We often do not realize how loud we are, do we? Unfortunately, Mike walked by the house of a neighbor who often gave our crew a hard time. She came walking toward him and when he realized she was, he took off his headphones and acknowledged her. She expressed her concern over the music he was singing and asked that he not do so. He immediately apologized and stated that he did not realize he was being loud. She continued to berate him in an extremely disrespectful way, telling him she was going to call the police. Again, he apologized and walked off as she continued to yell. He walked into the house even more frustrated than he was when he left.

It is unfortunate that kids just cannot be kids. Somehow, people know that we are a foster home. While I am sure it is often sensed because of the mix of races in our home, it is unacceptable to treat young people differently whether it is racially based or because they are or were in the foster care system. I have had people look at me and treat me in strange ways even at the grocery store when I have my kids, and it just is uncalled for.

I am asking my neighbors and you, my readers, to please give these young people a chance. They have been rejected and turned away by so many people in their lives and they do not deserve to be made uncomfortable in our neighborhoods. We do not look at and treat your kids the way that you do them. Please give them a chance and realize they are really trying to make a difference for themselves. They are not doing anything to bother or harm anybody and have absolutely no intention to do so. Try talking to them and developing a relationship, they are not going to bite.

These young adults are also going to make the same mistakes that you have made. Recently, one of my boys accidentally hit some trash cans on a street just outside our subdivision because he looked down at his phone. You would have thought he had torn out the whole block the way people carried on on social media pages. They talked about wanting to shut down the halfway house and started blaming everything on individuals in our home. It was so disheartening.

Yes, mistakes are going to be made. This message is short, but it needs to be heard and strong, stop judging. Judging, causes things to get worse rather than better as it creates a defensive wall and one of not being able to trust, building upon the years of experiences they have already had. This population and generation need adults who are going to support and encourage them, giving them grace and forgiveness. Rather than berate them, get to know them and make a difference in their lives, and yours.

Chapter 17
Do not Give Up On Me

As you can see from all these stories, love is not enough.

While foster parenting and helping these young adults is the hardest thing I have done, it is the best thing I have ever done with my life. Even through these challenges and events, I would not choose anything different. Each experience has made me and them better people, and together we will get to that side of victory and success.

This chapter is a plea to everyone. The young adults, foster parents, and the community. I am saddened by the number of kids who are removed from their homes when they turn 18. This needs to change as they are not ready to be on their own, even if they think they are. I cannot tell you how many young adults I have had conversations with who express how excited and ready they were to be adults and on their own, but now they wish they were not.

Let me start with you, the young adult. Do not give up on yourself, your foster parents, or your workers. I know that it is frustrating, and you just want to be independent but use this time to learn from them. Even if it feels like they do not know what they are talking about, or sometimes like they do not care. Take what you can and use the experiences to learn. Use this time to begin to advocate for yourself and know that you are not alone. There is a whole community of young adults who have made that transition and will stand beside you.

I also do not want you to give up on yourself. I am sorry that you have been through such circumstances and that it is hard to trust anybody. First, know that it is important to learn to trust and love yourself. The trajectory of your life depends on you and you alone. Having the determination to make decisions for yourself is empowering and helps you feel like you are in control, which you should be. Do not let anybody tell you that you cannot pursue your dreams. Your dreams are there for a reason. You are going to make mistakes, we all do. Just pick yourself up and learn from each experience, whether positive or negative. Do not give up. Know that I believe in you, wherever you are on your path.

You are amazing. You are strong and you can get through this. Many people want to help you. I know it is scary and trust comes hard but just keep trusting and soon you will find someone to love, support, and encourage you on your journey. Know that your journey is your own. It does not need to look like anybody else's. You are amazing and you will get there.

To foster parents. Please hear me on this. Do not give up on these individuals. They need you. You will have many different faces come to you. These faces come one person at a time. Their lives are complex and our work with them will be complex as well. You will need to be patient and supportive, pulling out all the tools you possess, maybe even learning some new ones as you help them grow and learn.

Believe me, I know how challenging it can be. But know that your support greatly increases their likelihood of success. Do not you want to see them be successful? I am sure that some of you have already faced major challenges and you are ready for them to be gone but try to see what is causing those challenges. It is probably fear or rejection. They need somebody willing to stand beside them through the good and the bad. For some, you are all they have.

Putting them out on their own before they are ready is just another rejection that they are going to have to overcome. You can do this. The payback you get by seeing their successes will far outweigh the challenges you have faced.

Do not let them go without ensuring they know you believe in them. Your belief will help them to believe in themselves.

Teach them tools for success and do not be afraid to let them start making decisions for themselves. How else are they going to learn? They need the safety net, whether they admit to it or not. You know what it is like in this world, and it is not as easy as it appears to an 18-year-old who is anxious to face life independently. You too, are not alone.

And last, to our community. Please try to understand this population. Realize that they are not here through their choices. Know that they each have their own needs and dreams. When you are looking into the face of one of these young adults, ask yourself how you would handle the situation if this were your child standing in front of you. Instead of looking down on them or judging them because of their circumstances, reach out to encourage and support them. You will be amazed at the person behind the masks they wear for protection.

There is a real need in this area, and we need to step up together to provide solutions and support to this population. I would throw a bunch of statistics out here, but those statistics change from year to year. What you need to know is that more than 50% of the young people who age out of foster care end up in homeless shelters or prisons within the first year. More than 50% end up having babies in their first year, as well. The percentage of those babies that end up in foster care as well is high. Let us break these trends by providing supportive family environments for young adults, helping them to be successful and break generational family patterns.

Over the years I have learned, that in addition to love, it takes a lot of essential skills. The first is patience. I often hear comments about not asking God for patience because He will surely test you. I can tell you, just get some kids and they will test you.

Patience also sometimes requires a very thick skin. We must learn that things often do not go at the pace we want. We need to be able to take things day to day. It also means we need to be able and willing to support individuals even when we may not agree with what they are doing. They need to discover their own way.

You also need that tough skin so that you do not react to things they say. More often than not, the words and things said at the moment are said because they feel safe with you. Many times, these words are not really directed at you, they are a product of years of hurt and not about you.

Family is so important. We need to provide a safe place to help individuals know that they belong and that they are not alone in their situation. They must know other young adults are going through the same thing. They need the comfort of knowing that when they make decisions, they have people who are there for them, cheering them on and helping provide redirection without dictating. Providing stability and support throughout this journey goes far. Let us sit back and watch as they discover themselves, take off their masks, and learn to love themselves. It all starts with love, but that is only the beginning. With love, patience, and lots of tools, we can help each one discover success.

Made in the USA
Middletown, DE
12 April 2024